Reclaiming Work

For Dorine
again, again and evermore

Reclaiming Work

Beyond the Wage-Based Society

ANDRÉ GORZ

Translated by Chris Turner

Polity Press

First published in 1999 by Polity Press in association with
Blackwell Publishers Ltd.
Published with the assistance of the French Ministry of Culture –
Centre National du Livre.

Reprinted 2005

Polity Press
65 Bridge Street
Cambridge CB2 1UR, UK

Polity Press
350 Main Street
Malden, MA 02148, USA

ISBN 0-7456-2127-9
ISBN 0-7456-2128-7 (pbk)

A catalogue record for this book is available from the British Library and
has been applied for from the Library of Congress.

Typeset in 11 on 13 pt Berling
by Best-set Typesetter Ltd., Hong Kong
Printed and bound in Great Britain by Marston Book Services Limited, Oxford

This book is printed on acid-free paper.

For further information on Polity, visit our website: www.polity.co.uk

Contents

Introduction

We have to learn to discern the unrealized opportunities which lie dormant in the recesses of the present. We must want to seize these opportunities, to take possession of the changes that are occurring. We must be bold enough to choose the Exodus. There is nothing to be gained from symptomatic treatments of the 'crisis', for there no longer is any crisis. A new system has been established which is abolishing 'work' on a massive scale. It is restoring the worst forms of domination, subjugation and exploitation by forcing each to fight against all in order to obtain the 'work' it is abolishing. It is not this abolition we should object to, but its claiming to perpetuate that same work, the norms, dignity and availability of which it is abolishing, as an obligation, as a norm, and as the irreplaceable foundation of the rights and dignity of all.

We must dare to prepare ourselves for the Exodus from 'work-based society': it no longer exists and will not return. We must want this society, which is in its death-throes, to die, so that another may arise from its ruins. We must learn to make out the contours of that other society beneath the resistances, dysfunctions and impasses which make up the present. 'Work' must lose its centrality in the minds, thoughts and imaginations of everyone. We must learn to see it differently: no longer as something we have – or do not have – but as *what we do*. We must be bold enough to regain control of the work we do.

The polemics stirred up by Jeremy Rifkin's book, *The End of Work*, are significant here.[1] What he calls the 'end of work' is the end of what everyone has become accustomed to call 'work'. It is not work in the anthropological or philosophical sense of the term. It is not the labour of the parturient woman, nor the work of the sculptor or poet. It is not work as the 'autonomous activity of transforming matter', nor as the 'practico-sensory activity' by which the subject exteriorizes him/herself by producing an object which bears his/her imprint. It is, unambiguously, the specific 'work' peculiar to industrial capitalism: the work we are referring to when we say 'she doesn't work' of a woman who devotes her time to bringing up her own children, but 'she works' of one who gives even some small part of her time to bringing up other people's children in a playgroup or a nursery school.

The 'work' one does in this sense (though it is more a 'having' than a 'doing': we speak of 'having a job') may have none of the characteristics of work in the anthropological or philosophical sense. Today, in fact, it is most often bereft of what defined work for Hegel: it is not the exteriorization (*Entäusserung*) by which subjects achieve self-realization by inscribing themselves upon the objective materiality of what they create or produce. The millions of clerical or technical workers 'working' on VDUs are not realizing anything tangible. Their practico-sensory activity is reduced to the barest minimum, their bodies and sensibilities bracketed out of the operation. Their 'work' is in no sense an 'appropriative shaping of the objective world', even though it may have such a shaping as a very distant and mediate effect. For the 'workers' in the 'intangible' sphere, and for a majority of service providers, the 'products' of their labour are evanescent, consumed at the same time as they are produced. Seldom can these 'workers' say: 'Here's what I've done. This is the piece of work I've made. This was my doing.' I hate the fraudsters who, in the name of the philosophical or anthropological definition of work, justify the value of a form of 'work' which is the very negation of that definition.

Efforts to deny 'the end of work' in the name of the necessity and permanence of work in the anthropological or philosophical sense demonstrate the opposite of what they were attempting to prove: it is precisely in the sense of self-realization, in the sense of '*poiesis*', of the creation of a work as *oeuvre*, that work is disappearing fastest into the virtualized realities of the intangible economy. If we wish to rescue and sustain this 'real work', it is urgent that we recognize that *real work is no longer what we do when 'at work'*: the work, in the sense of *poiesis*, which one *does* is no longer (or is increasingly rarely) done 'at work'; it no longer corresponds to the 'work' which, in the social sense of the term, one 'has'. One cannot demonstrate that 'the work-based society' must exist in perpetuity by invoking its anthropologically necessary character. In fact, the opposite is the case: we have to exit from 'work' and the 'work-based society' in order to recover a taste for, and the possibility of, 'true' work. Rifkin, in his way (which is not my own), is saying the same thing: the 'work' which he declares is coming to an end will have to be replaced by activities with other characteristics.

The 'work' capitalism is abolishing on a massive scale in its final phase is a social construction. It is for this very reason that it can be abolished. Why do we say that a woman 'works' when she takes care of children in a nursery school and 'does not work' when she stays at home to take care of her own children? Is it because the one is paid and the other not? But the mother at home would still not 'work' if she received an allowance equal to the wages of a nursery school teacher. She would not 'work' even if she too had a teaching qualification. Why is this? Because 'work' is defined from the outset as a *social* activity, marked out as forming part of the flow of social exchanges on a society-wide basis. The remuneration of this 'work' confirms its insertion into that flow, but that is not essential either: the essential point is that 'work' performs a *socially identified and normalized function in the production and reproduction of the social whole*. And to perform a socially identifiable function, it has itself to be identifiable by the *socially defined skills* it deploys, according to *socially determined procedures*. In other words, it has to be a 'job', a 'profession': that is to say, *the deployment of institutionally certified skills according to approved procedures*. None of these conditions is fulfilled by the housewife-and-mother: her work is not part of the process of social labour; it is not subject to approved procedures, institutionally monitored for their conformity to professional standards (or susceptible of such monitoring); it is not subject to public criteria in terms of hours and efficiency. In short, it is not in the public sphere, it does not meet socially codified, *socially defined needs*. This is something it shares with the work of slaves or personal servants who wait upon the personal desires of their master, not to mention the work of artistic or theoretical creation.

The theoretical or artistic creator 'works' (is 'in work') only when he/she is teaching or lecturing, satisfying a publicly and socially determined demand, or when he/she is fulfilling a commission. It is the same for all artistic, sporting or philosophical activities, the aim of which is the creation of meaning, of self (subjectivity), of knowledge. Creation is not socializable or codifiable: it is, in its essence, a transgression and recreation of norms and codes; it is solitude and rebellion, and contestation of 'work'. It cannot be a substitute for 'work', as Bernard Perret has suggested:[2] it cannot be an activity entrusted with the task of perpetuating work-based society.

By the social ratification of skills, procedures and needs it involves, 'work' is a powerful means of socialization, normalization and standardization, repressing or limiting both the individual and the collective invention, creation or self-determination of new norms, needs and skills. This is why the social recognition of new activities and competences meeting new needs has always had to be won through social struggles. The issue has always been, at least implicitly, a political one: society's grip – the power of its apparatuses, organized professions, laws and regulations – over the social actors had to be loosened in order for those actors to assert their power over society.

This in part explains the ease with which neo-liberalism gained acceptance from the end of the 1970s onwards. There was an increasingly widespread rejection, including within the working class, of the normalization inherent in Fordism and the 'dictatorship over needs' (Agnes Heller) inherent in the bureaucratism of the welfare state, in which citizens had become objects of state policy and had welfare rights only in so far as their cases fitted into a pre-established classification and an official categorization of needs. In this way, collective solutions to collective problems and the collective satisfaction of collective needs were ruled out, and relations of lived solidarity were broken down by a methodological individualism, which reinforced the domination by the state apparatus of citizens who had been transformed into its 'clients'.[3]

In principle (but in principle only), the massive abolition of 'work', its post-Fordist destandardization and demassification, the destatization and debureaucratization of social protection, could and should have opened up the social space for a proliferation of self-organized and self-determined activities, aimed at satisfying felt and self-defined needs. This liberation of work and expansion of the public sphere did not take place: they would have required the emergence of a different civilization, society and economy, putting an end to the power of capital over labour and to the pre-eminence of the criteria of financial profitability. Now, post-Fordist destandardization, demassification and debureaucratization pursued the opposite aim: substituting the anonymous 'laws' of the market for the laws which state-societies lay down for themselves; moving capital, through the unfettered play of these 'laws', beyond the power of the political sphere; bringing rebellious working classes into line by abolishing 'work', while continuing to make 'work' the basis of social belonging and rights, and the obligatory path to self-esteem and the esteem of others.

This is how a new era began, in which changes that could have served to liberate men and women from needs and servitude were turned round against them. This is how the same forms of subproletarianization, of psychological misery, of 'vagrancy' and 'brigandage' which accompanied the birth of manufacturing capitalism at the end of the eighteenth century reappeared. This is how third-world living conditions spread into the 'first world'. This is how the 'development' of forms of production which valorize capital caused that subsistence labour which does not valorize any to wither away, forcing hundreds of millions (this is no exaggeration) of country-dwellers in the 'third world' to swell the shanty-towns of the gigantic conurbations. This is how, at the same time, a historically unprecedented mass of capital obtained historically unprecedented rates of profit; and how that capital managed to achieve growing volumes of wealth-production while consuming less and less labour, distributing less and less in wages, paying less and less in taxes on its profits (even, indeed, no taxes at all) and, by so doing, ceasing to finance the social and environmental costs engendered by production, the cost of the infrastructures it requires.

This is how the material and cultural reproduction of societies has come into crisis, and how anomie, barbarism and 'civil' wars – latent or otherwise – have spread to all continents, together with the fear of a collapse of civilization and the implosion of the globalized, financialized economy, in which money makes money without buying or selling anything other than itself. Money has become a parasite devouring the economy, capital a predator pillaging society. Thanks to the globalization of the market, cut free from all rules and restrictions, both money and capital have cut themselves free from states and societies, substituting for state-societies an absolute non-society, and for nation-states a 'virtual' state that has no territory, borders, distances or citizens: King Money's own world-state. This is how capital has at last realized its ideal essence as supreme power admitting of neither division nor restriction. Capital, detached from the world of lived and sensible realities, has substituted the categorical imperative of its own growth for the criteria of human judgement and has put its own power beyond human grasp: it has achieved its Exodus.

Capitalism has managed in this way to overcome the crisis of the Fordist model. It has managed this by seizing upon a techno-scientific mutation *which exceeds its own grasp and whose historical and anthropological significance it is incapable of taking on board, as Jacques Robin has shown.*[4] It has largely de-materialized the main productive forces: labour (and we are only at the beginning of this process) and fixed capital. The most important form of fixed capital is now the knowledge stored in, and instantly available from, information technologies, and the most important form of labour power is brainpower. Between brainpower and fixed capital – in other words, between living knowledge and machine-knowledge – there is no longer any distinct boundary. Post-Fordist capitalism has taken over Stalin's formula: 'man is the most precious capital'. 'Man' is subsumed within the production process as 'human resource', as 'human capital', as fixed human capital. His specifically human capacities are integrated into a single system with the inanimate brainpower of machines. He has become a cyborg, a means of production in his totality – even in his subject-being. That is to say, he is capital, commodity and labour all rolled into one. And in so far as there is no use for his capacities in the system of valorization of money-capital, he is rejected, excluded, counted as non-existent. Man-as-most-precious-capital is only man if he can function as capital.

This provides a context for Lester Thurow's excellent question: 'How is capitalism to function when the most important types of capital [knowledge capital] cannot be owned?'[5] For the moment, capitalism offers two partial, provisional answers:

1 The 'individual enterprise', in which 'man' treats himself as capital and valorizes himself as such. This is the case with the 'elite of knowledge workers', as Rifkin calls them, who form part of the 4 per cent of American workers who together earn as much as half (51 per cent) of all employed persons. They are a small elite of prosperous Americans enjoying 'an affluent lifestyle far removed from the social turmoil around them'. Indeed, the members of this 'high-tech nomadic tribe . . . have more in common with each other than with the citizens of whatever country they happen to be doing business in.' And the expectation, as former US Secretary of Labor Robert Reich argues, must be that they will 'withdraw into ever more isolated enclaves . . . and the symbolic-analytical zones where they work will bear no resemblance to the rest of America'.[6]

2 The second solution is the one proposed by the big corporations: they take possession of 'human capital' by re-establishing pre-capitalist – and, indeed, almost feudal – relations of vassalage and allegiance. We shall return to this question below.

Capitalism will avoid collapse, writes Thurow, only if it changes fundamentally, proposes a 'grand agenda', 'a compelling vision of a better future', a 'vision that underlies some common goals that members of a society can work together to achieve'. But this vision, he adds, is nowhere in existence as yet: it is the job of the left 'to have a utopian vision of the future that provides the locomotive power for change'.[7] Must capitalism be saved in spite of itself, then? And is this possible? Isn't there something better we could do? Can we respond to its Exodus by ourselves departing to terrains it does not dominate? Are there practicable ways to achieve that Exodus in both the rich and the peripheral countries, which currently have 800 million people totally or partially unemployed and where 1,200 million young people will come on to the labour market in the next twenty-five years?

Some of us in the early sixties made a distinction between subordinate and revolutionary reforms.[8] The former are predicated on the urgent need to remedy the dysfunctions of existing society, the latter on the need to pass beyond existing society towards a different one that is currently in gestation, a society which provides a meaning and ultimate goal for action. The task of politics here is to define intermediate strategic objectives, the pursuit of which meets the urgent needs of the present while at the same time prefiguring the alternative society that is asking to be born.

I find the same approach today in the work of Henri Maler[9] and in that of Jacques Bidet, with whom I feel the greatest affinity. 'When you have given up acting on the basis of a radically different final goal,' the latter writes, 'there's a danger that the precise boundary-line between the socialist transformation of capitalist society and mere adjustments to capitalism will be obliterated . . . It is reasonable to assess the way the world is moving on the basis of its ultimate conceivable state . . . The only ones who will be heard in the end are those who wish to change the face of the earth.'[10]

1

From the Social State to the Capital State

Laissez-faire too is a form of State regulation, introduced and maintained by legislative and coercive means. It is a deliberate policy,
conscious of its own ends and not the spontaneous, automatic
expression of economic facts.

Antonio Gramsci[1]

THE GREAT REFUSAL

'One could argue that the capitalists had declared class warfare on
labour and were winning,' writes Lester Thurow.[2] This is not a bad
way to approach our subject. Globalization cannot, in fact, be explained by the information technology revolution or by the search
for new commercial outlets. At the beginning it was an essentially
political response to what, towards the middle of the 1970s, was
called 'the crisis of governability'. That crisis, the chief preoccupation of the public and private decision-makers grouped together in
the Trilateral Commission, showed itself at all levels of society: at
the state level, in schools and universities, in companies, towns and
cities, in hospitals and in all those apparatuses which were supposed
to ensure the cultural reproduction of society.

In the United States the crisis assumed quasi-insurrectional forms
from 1964 onwards. Rioting by the black proletariat, spreading from
east to west, had sacked and burned whole districts of cities – in

Detroit the uprising had lasted a week – and had continued into the seventies in the form of mass rebellion and sabotage in the big factories and the universities. By 1967, the 'dissidence' had reached the universities and secondary schools of West Germany. It then spread into the industrial centres of the rest of Europe and was continued into the middle of the 1970s (until 1980 in Italy) in the form of industrial action radically different from the customary strikes: rejection of imposed work rhythms; rejection of wage differentials; refusal to kow-tow to bullying foremen; self-ordained reductions in the pace of work; lengthy occupations in which bosses or trade-union leaders were held against their will; refusal to delegate negotiating power to the legal representatives of the workforce; refusal to compromise over grassroots demands; and, quite simply, refusal to work.

These were all so many ways of refusing to accept not just the oppressive organization of the big factories, large-scale offices and big department stores, but the permanent, quasi-institutional pursuit of class compromise – a pursuit which was the very cornerstone of the 'Fordist compromise'. The social movements of the years 1967–74 consciously took their stand away from the terrain marked out by the institutions of the state-society. Instead of making demands, they sought to change 'life' for themselves – to change what conditioned it and what it was made up of. To change it by taking it outside the logic of productivity, but also outside the logic of abstract labour, standardization, mass consumption, normality, quantification and synchronization. To change it by asserting the specificity of needs and desires which cannot possibly be satisfied monetarily or in commodity form.[3] 'The feminists' protest goes much further than the ecologists',' write Pietro Ingrao and Rossana Rossanda.

> The political sphere stands accused by the feminist campaign of being an arena with essentially masculine, essentially productivist parameters, and hence parameters which are competitive and war-like, which take no account of the body, reproduction and the emotions . . . the body, sex . . . powerfully resisting legal abstraction, resisting that *reductio ad unum* which denies dissymmetry and is the basis of masculine culture and power.[4]

Contrary to the forecasts of the founders of the welfare state, social protection and benefits had not reconciled populations with capitalist society, nor had the procedures for permanent negotiation and arbitration defused social antagonisms. In fact, the opposite was the case. By intervening, regulating, protecting and arbitrating in all fields, the state had substituted itself for whole swathes of civil society and had subsumed it: it had put itself in the front line. Being responsible for everything – or almost everything – it had become vulnerable by the very scope of its functions. It was, therefore, urgent – and this was the unspoken agenda of the Trilateral Commission – to substitute for this over-visible and too easily assailable organizing mechanism an invisible and anonymous one whose unauthored laws would be irresistibly imposed on everyone by force of circumstance as 'laws of nature'. The mechanism in question was the market.

The same line of reasoning was applied to the 'crisis of governability' afflicting companies. The gigantic scale of the great factories and administrations typical of Fordism, and the centralized, hierarchical, rigid organization of compartmentalized tasks, of work broken down into minutely fragmented operations co-ordinated by a host of officers and NCOs of production, made companies extremely vulnerable. There too it became urgent to replace the over-visible power of the central organizing mechanism with forms of de-centred self-organization, or, in other words, with the creation of a network of relatively autonomous sub-units which, in taking over their own co-ordination, would also make for a saving in organizational costs. It was urgent to break the combativeness of the workers, to smash the trade unions' negotiating power, to remove the 'rigidities' which collective bargaining, factory agreements and welfare rights had introduced into the relations of production. In a word, the labour market had to be 'liberated' from the elements which were 'distorting' it. The watchword was 'deregulate'.

THE 'EXODUS' OF CAPITAL

The 'crisis of governability' afflicting both societies and companies was the sign that a particular model had had its day. For almost thirty years Western governments had pursued Keynesian, *dirigiste* policies in which the state stimulated the growth of production and demand by fiscal and monetary measures, redistributed an increasing proportion of the wealth produced, and created as many jobs through public expenditure as increased productivity eliminated in the private sector. Now, from the early seventies onwards, the expansion of economies began to run up against limits which could not be surmounted by policies for supporting and stimulating growth. Internal markets were saturated and could provide no justification for investments in new capacity. The 'marginal productivity of capital' (that is to say, the additional profits ensuing from additional investment) was tending towards zero and its collapse presaged the end of an era in which production, demand, productivity and profits had been able to grow harmoniously.

With the slow-down in economic expansion, one tended also to see a dramatic downturn in economies of scale and in productivity gains. From this point on, the Keynesian state and Keynesian policies presented more disadvantages for capitalism than advantages. In the absence of significant economic growth, they increased the burden of the state and its sway over society. In the countries with the most advanced social policies, public expenditure approached, and in some cases exceeded, 70 per cent of GDP, while budget deficits ran to 10 per cent and more. The Meidner Plan, which the Swedish Social-Democratic Party adopted, showed that the private ownership of capital was no longer inviolate: the plan was for the welfare funds managed by the trade unions gradually to buy up the country's main companies and develop them as workers' co-operatives, in keeping with the vision of a social-democratic civilization.

Capital, fearing it was under threat of socialization or state takeover, felt well advised to put an end to its symbiosis with a state which had become incapable of ensuring the expansion of the internal market. Economic planning or tripartite dialogue had been useful only during the period of 'extensive growth' in which lower unit costs had been achieved by mass production with longer and longer product runs in ever more gigantic plants. At that stage industry had to plan its investments far in advance and needed a state that was also planning the essential infrastructures and public services far ahead. With the slow-down or halting of growth, it was no longer planning (a source of rigidities), but the utmost possible mobility and flexibility that were the key to increasing or maintaining market share. The 'competitive imperative' and the concern to re-establish 'governability' both pointed in the same direction. Capital had to free itself from its dependence on the state and relax the social constraints it was under. The state had to be made to serve the 'competitiveness' of companies by accepting the supremacy of 'market laws'. The turnabout in the balance of forces would follow naturally.

The flight of capital did, in fact, gather momentum from the beginning of the seventies with the development of what were then called 'multinationals' – firms which set up producer subsidiaries in foreign countries so as to be able to access those countries' internal markets. At that point the great majority of multinationals were American. This was a far cry from the globalization which occurred around 1990, as the free movement of goods was still limited by trade barriers, and capital transfers were subject to control and prior authorization by states. It would not be until the end of the seventies that these obstacles to mobility were progressively abolished, under pressure from the big corporations. From multinational companies they would then turn into truly transnational, global corporations.

The argument was the same everywhere: corporations had a good chance of achieving continued growth only if they succeeded in increasing their exports, that is to say, in increasing their share of the world market. And the expansion of their market share required the liberalization not only of the trade in goods, but also of capital flows; it required the possibility of investing and producing abroad, of borrowing in foreign financial markets on the most favourable terms. In the competition between the corporations, those subject to fewest controls and limits on their freedom of movement were most likely to come out on top. The 'competitive imperative' led inexorably to the globalization of the economy and the divorce between the interests of capital and those of the nation-state. The *political space* (of states) and the *economic space* (of capitalist corporations) *could no longer coincide*. It was the end of what Robert Reich has termed 'economic nationalism'.

Globalization could not have developed, nor even have been envisaged, in the absence of the potential of 'information technologies', which had until then lain largely unexploited. Were it not that each corporation could hope to gain additional shares of the world market by exploiting the latent possibilities of the information technology revolution better and more quickly than the others, the tendency towards cartelization and the division of the world by cartel agreements would probably have prevailed (as in the thirties) over the

'trade wars' which led to globalization. We should, however, beware
of linear explanations. The information technology revolution made
globalization possible. But, conversely, globalization enabled – then
required – the accelerated development of the information technologies and their applications. Capital needed a technical revolution to overcome the crisis of Fordism, free itself from the constraints
of the social state, reduce unit labour costs and speed up productivity growth. But that technical revolution could only be set in train
if the relation of social forces and the relation of forces between
capital and the state were at the same time, and irresistibly, modified
in favour of capital.

What made the Exodus of capital possible also in the end made
it necessary. The 'transnationalization' of companies, their Exodus
from the national political space, was becoming a 'survival imperative' for every one of them. They had to stop being enterprises and
become 'global players', co-ordinating and linking a wide diversity
of markets and suppliers of all sizes world-wide. Robert Reich quotes
the example of a Pontiac Le Mans, where 30 per cent of production
costs go to assembly shops in South Korea, 17.5 per cent to Japanese engine-builders, electronics experts and parts manufacturers, 7.5
per cent to German designers, 4 per cent to Taiwan, Singapore and
Japan for small components and 3 per cent to Great Britain, Ireland
and Barbados for computer services and marketing.

THE END OF ECONOMIC NATIONALISM

The company is a transnational network and its co-ordination and
strategic decision-making centre has a nationality only in appearance,
as a by-product of its origins. The registered offices can be anywhere
at all. Through transfer pricing, the company makes its profits wherever it pays the lowest taxes – or no taxes at all. It negotiates with
nation-states as one power with another, plays them off against each
other and sets up its production units in the places where it gets the
largest subsidies and tax breaks, the best infrastructure, and a disci-
plined and cheap workforce. In this way, it gains for itself a kind
of extra-territoriality, divesting the nation-state of those two attributes of sovereignty: the power to raise taxes and the power to set
the rate at which they are raised. 'Capital is now the "sole posses-
sor" of sovereignty,' writes Marco Revelli, 'being able to lord it over

nations and decide their fates' and 'dictate its own rules to the former sovereign'.[5]

Never before had capitalism managed to free itself so completely from political power. But we should note that it is only nation-states that are circumvented in this way. And that it has only succeeded in dominating them by establishing an omnipresent, supra-national state with its own institutions, apparatuses and networks of influence. Those institutions are, of course, the WTO (ex-GATT), the IMF, the World Bank and the OECD. They it is that formulate and enforce the binding regulations and laws of free competition and the free circulation of goods and capital, and that propagate the neo-liberal credo that all problems are best resolved by allowing free rein to the laws of the market.

With the supra-national state of capital we see for the first time a state free of any territoriality, whose power, though it is imposed from outside on territorialized states, does not recreate any other political arena outside of them. It is, rather, independent and separated from any society. It is situated in a non-place, whence it limits and regulates the power of societies to determine what happens in *their* places. Without either a social base or a political constitution, it is a pure apparatus expressing the rights of globalized capital. Being itself a power without a society, it tends to engender societies without power. It throws states into crisis, discredits politics, imposing its demands for mobility, 'flexibility', privatization and deregulation, lower public expenditure, and reduced social costs and wages, which are all allegedly indispensable for the free operation of the law of the market.

The denationalization of economies inevitably runs up against resistance (ineffective because it is merely national), which splits both the political right and left down the middle. On the one hand, there is the globalist, neo-liberal, ideologically (if not politically) pro-American bourgeoisie, which favours diluting the European Union to make it a free trade area with America; on the other side there are the traditional industries and bourgeoisies, the pre-capitalist strata and some of the trade unions. Ranged against the unified onslaught of globalizing capital we have, then, the disordered resistance of antagonistic strata and classes running from the extreme right to the extreme left, who can generally find little with which to oppose capital's globalism except various forms of national conservatism or statism.

Now, rejecting globalization *as such*, seeking to resist it nationally, leads inevitably to capitulation in the face of *this particular form of globalization*. We should not be fighting globalization as such, seeking to pull back from it; we should rather be fighting, within the context of the current globalization, for a different form of globalization. Resistance to transnational capital can only be transnational itself; resistance to the forces bringing about this globalization demands first and foremost people who can bring about *a different globalization*, based on worldwide solidarity and vision, on a new blueprint for the civilization of the planet. States are not without the requisite levers for changing the direction and nature of globalization. But they do not possess them individually. They will not have them so long as they lack the common political will to win back through common action what can now only be a pooled sovereignty. The irresistible power of global capital is due above all to the inclination of states to compete against each other to attract capital by granting it favours, rather than to stand together and refuse to be played off against each other. We shall see below that the impotence of nation-states is not merely a passive matter: it is also used as an excuse to re-establish privileges which Fordism had eaten into and to abolish rights it had established.

'BLAME IT ON GLOBALIZATION'

Globalization and the intensified competition in every market in every country are used as all-purpose justifications: for the fall in real wages, the dismantling of social welfare systems, spiralling unemployment, generalized job insecurity, deteriorating working conditions and so on. We are told these things are all inevitable and necessary. It is like this, explains Pierre-Noël Giraud, with irrefutable logic, because the ability of companies to compete depends on their investments in productivity. 'They have to have broadly the same rates of investment' to remain competitive. 'This means that the wage/profit distribution can no longer be decided on economic policy criteria, but that . . . *the territory which has the distribution most favourable to profits*, and hence the highest potential growth [of investment] *will set the standard.*'[6]

In other words, to be able to meet competition from American and Japanese firms, for example, European companies will have to achieve American or Japanese rates of profit. This formally correct argument would apply, however, only if companies' rates of investment were equal to their rates of profit or, in other words, if all profits were reinvested. But what happens in reality is actually quite different.

In the 1980s, thanks to 're-engineering', the pre-tax profits of the 500 largest American companies rose on average by 92 per cent. In 1987, 61 per cent of those profits (as against 22 per cent in 1953) went to the chief executive officers (CEOs) of those firms and in many cases the dividends paid to shareholders increased fourfold. Two-thirds of American economic growth went into the pockets of 1 per cent of the working population.[7] In 1994, a CEO earned on average 187 times as much as a blue- or white-collar worker. In 1975 he earned 'only' 41 times as much and in 1992 'only' 145 times as much.[8] The same trend has also been seen in the rest of the world.

In France, for example, the tax breaks on financial earnings between 1989 and 1991 deprived the state coffers of an annual 80 billion francs of revenue. Throughout the world, it was solemnly explained that 'the competitive imperative' demanded a reduction in the taxes on high incomes, since it was the savings of the rich which (in part) financed the investment essential to business competitiveness. But that investment has not occurred. And not just in America. In France the rate of investment by companies fell to its lowest level for 35 years in 1995, when it was 16.2 per cent, as against 19.4 per cent in 1980 and 21.6 per cent in 1970. Since 1992, total profits have invariably been higher than total investment. They were 71 billion francs higher in 1993, 102 billion higher in 1995 and 127 billion higher in 1997 – 127 billion earned from 'downsizing', 'restructuring', from making jobs more 'flexible' and more insecure; 127 billion francs sterilized, by being 'invested' – if you can call it that – on the financial markets.

In Germany in 1978 net wages represented 54 per cent of national disposable income; unearned income represented 22 per cent and welfare benefits and pensions 23 per cent. In 1994, the share of wages had fallen to 45 per cent (a drop of 17 per cent), with profits and unearned income rising to 33 per cent (a 50 per cent increase). Adjusting for inflation, profits rose by 90 per cent between 1979 and 1994 and wages by 6 per cent, but the share of taxes on profits in total tax receipts fell by a half during these fifteen years, dropping from 25 to 13 per cent. It was 35 per cent in 1960 in a period of strong economic expansion.

Was it, in fact, the pressure of international competition which required these changes? Is it not, rather, that such competition provided an alibi for redistributing income from the poorest to the richest and for onslaughts on the 'welfare state' and the 'featherbedding' of wage-earners? How can international competition explain French publishers putting out their books to be typeset in Madagascar, Tunisia or Mauritius? Is it to make a few pennies on the price of a book? And is it to meet competition that gentlemen's shirtmakers have garments made up in China which are then sold at 50–100 times their cost price? Or that Nike (or Reebok or Puma) have their shoes manufactured in the Philippines, then in Indonesia, before moving on to China and Vietnam where the wage costs for a pair of 'Pegasus' trainers which sell for 70 dollars are 1 dollar 66 cents – and that the fourteen American board members of Nike have been able to pick up an annual income equal to the wages of 18,000 women workers in the Philippines? Or that Ford immediately sacked the workforce of two of its Mexican subsidiaries for protesting against the 50-hour week forced on them in contravention of Mexican law? Why, to use Alain Lipietz's excellent phrase, does 'competitiveness' demand the lowest wage costs, while allowing the highest management costs?[9]

If we ask what transnational companies have done with their profits, we see they have certainly not invested them. In fact, their rates of investment have fallen by comparison with the levels of the sixties and seventies.[10] What has increased, and very greatly, by contrast, are the dividends to the shareholders, the remuneration of senior management and CEOs, and:

1   purchases of companies by other companies ('mergers'), which have given rise to transactions of 400–800 billion dollars a year, as against 20–40 billion in the early 1980s. The financing of these mergers has absorbed 90 per cent of the transnationals' foreign investment;[11]
2   purely financial 'investments', on the money and foreign exchange markets in particular, through which countless firms (including, among others, Siemens, which is the largest European corporation) earn more than they do from their productive activities.

'The competitive imperative' is a fine catch-all explanation; anything at all can be blamed on globalization. For the main players in that process, globalization is not a passively felt constraint, but an array of constraints they themselves impose in the service of their own global power. This power is being concentrated in fewer and fewer hands. Of the 37,000 transnationals which control 40 per cent of world trade and a third of conventionally quantifiable world production, 370 (1 per cent) control 50 per cent of the financial assets. According to the IMF, no more than fifty banks control all the daily transactions, amounting to 1.4 trillion dollars, on the foreign exchange markets. And just six chartered banks control 90 per cent of operations on derivatives.[12]

THE RESISTIBLE DICTATORSHIP OF THE FINANCIAL MARKETS

Financial logic is winning out over economic logic, rent is winning out over profit. Financial power, referred to euphemistically as 'the markets', is becoming independent of societies and the real economy, and is imposing its norms of profitability on businesses and states. The president of the Bundesbank, Hans Tietmeyer, said this clearly at Davos in February 1996: 'The financial markets will increasingly play the role of "policemen" . . . Politicians have to understand that they are now under the control of the financial markets and not, any longer, of national debates.'[13]

Into those financial markets, the American pension funds, which manage 8 trillion dollars, and investment funds have introduced a practice commonly known elsewhere as 'extortion' or, more colloquially, 'racketeering'. They choose a number of prosperous, highly priced companies, buy up sizeable quantities of their shares and then confront the boards of those companies with the following option: either give us a dividend of at least 10 per cent or we wreck your share price. That practice, which makes maximum short-term financial returns the highest imperative, has pushed up shareholder value to unprecedented levels.

In the light of these facts, the argument that an increase in public expenditure reduces 'the amount of savings likely to be lent to companies . . . and hence their capacity to defend their competitiveness' becomes laughable.[14] Denmark has a level of public expenditure equal to 62 per cent of GDP, a rate of mandatory contributions of

54 per cent of GDP, a 'wage floor' of more than £7 per hour, unemployment benefit equal to 90 per cent of earned income for up to five years and a negligible rate of youth unemployment, and yet it has one of the most prosperous and competitive economies in the world. By contrast, the United States, with one of the lowest rates of mandatory contributions, has also one of the lowest rates of saving, with its private citizens in debt to the tune of 60,000 dollars per household.

'One cannot see why the French worker would in the long run earn a great deal more than the Chinese who does the same as he/she does at a comparable level of productivity,' observes P.-N. Giraud.[15] But it is not clear either why, as Giraud asserts, workers should have 'only one alternative: either do what low-wage countries don't yet know how to do and, therefore, in my vocabulary, join the "competitive" group or enter the service of these latter', accepting lower wages.[16] Why should the increase within a given population of the proportion of 'competitive individuals', whose incomes are generally very much above the average, not be accompanied by fiscal redistribution? Why could not those people whose work has been transferred to Chinese workers be put to work, not for the 'competitive individuals' who would pay them personally for their services, but to satisfy the innumerable collective needs which go unmet because the community does not grant itself the means to pay for them collectively? Why do we have to go on lightening the tax load on higher incomes (including those of the 'competitive'), on financial earnings, on profits that are not reinvested?

The answer to these questions is not economic, but political and ideological. Tax breaks and reductions do not reflect economically rational choices. They merely indicate that national governments fight over the privilege of keeping on – or attracting to – their territories financial capital which moves at the speed of light between markets and currencies thousands of times a day in search of the maximum immediate profit. It is no longer a question for states of promoting productive investment; they are simply concerned to prevent or restrict the outflow of a capital that has no territory, or to attract, by fiscal dumping, social dumping and wage dumping, the head offices of transnationals, as Belgium and the Netherlands have done with their 'management centres'.[17]

The trend towards replacing social welfare systems by private insurance schemes and private pension funds (funded schemes) is part of this same logic – replacing redistribution through the tax system by private insurance; substituting private management by finance for social management of social welfare by the political system.[18]

I do not in any sense intend by these remarks to deny that social welfare systems need to be rethought and re-established on new foundations. I shall examine this question in chapter 4 below. My point is simply that the 'reforms' which are dismantling social welfare systems on the pretext that they are outdated 'social entitlements' which are no longer fundable for lack of resources are socially, politically and morally unacceptable. If those systems can no longer be funded, it is not because there is any lack of resources or because resources have to be directed as a priority to investment for increased productivity. If they can no longer be funded, it is because an increasing proportion of GDP is directed at remunerating capital and the proportion distributed to remunerate work has been constantly falling. Now, it is largely on this latter that the funding of social welfare payments falls. The social struggles to defend 'welfare rights' must be understood first and foremost as defending a principle: namely, that there are ultimate limits to capital's power over politics; ultimate limits to the rights of the economic sphere over society. The redefinition of social welfare provision is acceptable only when this principle is recognized. And the recognition of this principle implies and demands, above all, that societies regain power over their own destinies by putting an end, through concerted action, to the power financial capital has assumed over them.

As long ago as 1978, James Tobin, a winner of the Nobel prize for economics, recommended one element of this necessary action. In order to curb purely speculative operations on the financial markets, he advocated a tax of 0.1 per cent on all spot currency conversions.[19] In his view such a tax would reduce the volume of transactions by two-thirds and would bring states some 150 billion dollars of revenue a year. In 1995, in response to the objections levelled against his scheme, Tobin presented a new version of his proposal. The aim of this new version was to prevent the banks evading taxation on their operations by relocating – as they had threatened to do – in 'tax havens' or offshore. In this new version of the scheme, the various countries – and the European Union, in particular – would impose an additional tax (of 0.04 per cent) on any lending of their money to foreign finance houses, including the foreign subsidiaries of their own banks.[20] This tax would have a negligible effect on trade and investment; by contrast, it would restrict purely speculative operations, which exceed actual trade in goods by a factor of fifty, and would greatly reduce the capacities of the financial markets to influence the policies of states.

Clearly, further instruments will be needed to put an end to the dictatorship of finance capital. Above all, it will take a common political resolve on the part of states. The fact that the 'irresistible power of the markets' exists only as a result of governments' willing submission to the power of finance – which they then use as an alibi to carry forward on their own account the war capitalism has declared first on the working class and, thereafter, on society as a whole – will have to be understood and made manifest. Alain Lipietz is not the only one to show that 'an alternative Europe is possible, one in which there is social provision and solidarity', an alternative which would offer the world a new model of 'development', of society and of North–South relations.[21] As we shall see a little further on, Asia's 'opinion-formers' are currently considering this same idea. And Lester Thurow, once again, reminds us that the rules of world trade have always been laid down by the main trading power and that power today is – by a considerable distance – the European Union.[22] That body could gear itself up to present 'an alternative to Anglo-Saxon monetarist policies'. It could, adds Patrick Viveret, use the Euro as a lever to 'set an ecological and social model of development against the Anglo-Saxon laissez-faire model'.[23] It could transform North–South relations by levying what Lipietz calls 'socio-taxes' or 'eco-taxes' on imports, the yield from these being restored in full to the exporting countries of the South with both parties profiting.[24]

THE CHINESE MIRAGE

In the short or medium term, then, states are not without the requisite means (provided, of course, that they unite to use them) to break the stranglehold of deterritorialized capital, to regain increased measures of autonomy and to begin fundamental transformations of an economic, ecological and societal nature, which will lead to a transcending of the wage-based society. All that is lacking is the political will. I can already hear the objection that this concern

to leave wage-based society behind is typically a Western intellectual's indulgence, in an era when China and India are making great
strides forward into that form of society and experts are predicting
a new 'long wave' of economic expansion, driven by the '750 million
consumers' who, in Asia alone, will have a purchasing power equal
to that of the wage-earners in the rich countries by the year 2010.
The Asian market, it is said, will restore health and dynamism to
world capitalism and the Western economies. Refound growth
should drive down unemployment everywhere.[25]

Regarding such prognoses, we would do well here to heed the following comment by Rüdiger Machetzki, who begins by quoting from
a devastatingly ironic editorial in the *Asian Wall Street Journal* of 26
October 1995:

> 'The idea that the 21st century will be an Asian century is one of the
> stranger fantasies ever to grip the Western imagination.' To critical
> observers, it is gradually becoming clear that the productive capaci-
> ties of the region are growing much faster than the region's capacity
> to absorb its products. Too slow an increase in regional purchasing
> power is the inevitable concomitant of low production costs.[26]

In short, the conditions for endogenous growth are not met – to
the point, indeed, where Japan has since the early months of 1994
transferred more capital to the West than it has invested in Asia.

> When even Japanese experts are becoming alarmed that Japan is on
> the way to becoming 'a great power in unemployment terms' . . .
> thoughtful opinion-formers in the region are beginning to doubt
> whether the social and economic problems of Western Europe really
> are the effect of Western decadence (Eurosclerosis). They are now
> asking themselves whether these are not, rather, basic structural prob-
> lems of a global kind, which Asia itself will one day run up against.
> If jobless growth is not a specifically European problem but a global
> one, then Europe is in advance of other countries in its experience of
> this problem. The solutions will thus also have to come from Europe.[27]

There is no clearer way to put it: the return to virtual full employment through the creation of hundreds of millions of new Western-
ized consumers is a mirage. Industrialization on the Western model
and Fordist-type growth will not be reproduced throughout the rest
of the world. The economic strategy adopted by Western 'investors'

themselves rules out this possibility. To understand this, one has only to read the writings of Kenichi Ohmae, one of the most eminent strategists of the new model of capitalist development.[28] That model, the so-called 'Zebra Strategy', implies not the development of countries or territories but only – in China as elsewhere – of enclaves (some twenty of them), the income from which, in Ohmae's view, can become ten to twenty times higher per head of population than the income for the rest of the population. In a word, 'development' is not to be disseminated outside the enclaves; the wealth acquired within these will not be redistributed by the nation-state. Capitalism must be able to produce its own spatiality, separate from that of the nation; it will have to be able to wall itself up in 'city-states' and 'private towns' such as we already find in the USA, and carry on its 'private wars' against populations which have become nomadic and warlike as society has broken down. This represents a return to the 'shapeless, endemic wars that are difficult to stamp out', akin to the Mad-Max-style campaigns which the unstructured wars fought by the pillaging armies in Liberia and Mozambique have already begun to resemble.[29]

The model advocated by Ohmae is the very one that is taking shape today in China, India, Malaysia, Mexico, Brazil, etc. There, capitalism is propelling 'special economic zones' into the post-industrial era, zones which have to be defended from the outset not against 'immigration', but against internal migration or, in other words, against invasion by landless peasants, against the flight from the land.

The model of industrialization which enabled the West and Japan to develop no longer exists. The type of industrialization which enabled the rural masses to become urban wage-earners no longer exists. It is disappearing even in China, where traditional industry has become obsolete and uncompetitive – that traditional industry which, before the rise of 'market communism', gave jobs for life to 110 million wage-earners, thereby providing them with the so-called 'iron rice-bowl', that is to say, with a vital minimum in terms of food, housing and services.

The 100 million or so Chinese migrants who, like the 'vagabonds' and 'brigands' of the eighteenth century in Europe, rove from city to city and town to town in search of some way of making a living will have their numbers swelled by a further 300 million in the first decade of the twenty-first century. Current unemployment among the Chinese urban population is estimated by the International Labour Office at 17–20 per cent, with peaks of 34 per cent.[30] The 'special economic zones' in which the transnationals have set up operations employ 7 million people all told.[31] And extensive industrialization, the kind which creates huge numbers of jobs, has already exceeded the bounds of what is ecologically sustainable.

It has to be remembered that China, which has one-fifth of the world's population, has only 85 square metres of cultivable surface per inhabitant; that 40 per cent of cultivable surfaces have already been destroyed since 1955, 5 per cent by erosion and desertification, 35 per cent by urbanization and industrialization; that five of the ten most polluted cities in the world are in China; that China suffers from a dramatic water shortage; that half its water courses have been sterilized by industrial effluents and no longer support life; that bottled water is dearer than milk in Beijing and there are 'oxygen bars' selling pure air to consumers. It must be remembered also that two-thirds of the population and two-thirds of agriculture and industry are concentrated in valleys which are protected from flooding only by a continual raising of the level of dikes. One has to bear all this in mind to assess to what degree 'the talk of cars or personal computers for all is', as Jacques Robin writes, 'rendered absurd by global ecology'.[32]

One has also to remember that the figure for worldwide unemployment stands at between 600 and 800 million and that, if we were to extend the wage-based society to all who will enter the labour market between now and 2025, yet another 1,200 million jobs would have to be created.[33] One has to see that almost the entire (potential) rise in the world's working population (99 per cent) will take place among the poor (i.e. less than $120 per month), or very poor (less than $40 per month), populations of the so-called peripheral countries. And that transnationals' investment in these countries often creates more unemployment than jobs, and at any rate does not in any sense alleviate the extreme mass poverty. Ignacy Sachs points out, for example, that 'in the city of Campinas, one of the main technological centres of Latin America and a place responsible for 9 per cent of Brazilian GDP, 40 per cent of the inhabitants do not have sufficient income to purchase the adequate basket of consumer goods.'[34] Jeremy Rifkin shows that the subsidiaries of the transnationals in Brazil – like the *maquiladoras*, the industries which the big North American companies set up in the frontier regions of

Mexico – are often more automated than their equivalents in the United States. They distribute too little in wages to propel economic expansion by increasing effective demand. On the other hand, with the help of customs union, they open up the country to imported mass-produced goods, leading to the ruin of small local and craft industries.[35]

Finding alternatives to wage-based society is, then, no mere indulgence of decadent intellectuals in the rich countries. Wage-based society has less to offer humanity and the world than the social model of Kerala,[36] the technically advanced self-providing co-operatives in the agricultural villages of India which Alvin Toffler describes, or the 'high-tech self-providing' advocated by Frithjof Bergmann in the United States.[37]

I shall return to this question at greater length below, though I do not claim to be able to offer any ready-made solutions. The most urgent thing is to modify our vision, in order to learn to discern the seeds of other possible worlds within our own as it is dying and changing.

But before we come to these other aspects of change, we have to be properly informed about, and better grasp the nature of, the actors in – and possible subjects of – the transformations which are currently taking place.

2

The Latest Forms of Work

The end of 'Fordist' growth left companies with two ways of attempting to escape stagnation. They could either (1) win additional market share or (2) renew their product range at a faster rate and increase its built-in obsolescence. As regards the winning of additional market share, the prospects were more promising in relatively 'virgin' markets: firms thus had to try and gain a foothold in the 'emerging' countries. As for accelerated obsolescence, that required not only intense, sustained effort in terms of innovation, but also the capacity to produce in ever shorter product runs at lower and lower unit costs.

Both options necessarily entailed breaking with the Fordist mode of production. Competitiveness was no longer to depend on the economies of scale previously achieved by mass production. It was, rather, to be achieved by the capacity to produce an increasing variety of products on shorter and shorter time scales, in smaller quantities and at lower prices. Growth, which had been quantitative and material, was now to become 'qualitative' and 'immaterial'. It was now 'image', novelty and symbolic value that were to sell products. Competitiveness demanded maximum mobility, fluidity and rapidity in designing new products and putting them into production. Firms had to be capable of continual improvisation; they had to know how to whip up passing fads, unpredictable and transient fashions, and exploit them to the full. In virtually saturated markets, the only type of growth possible was growth in the variety of taste and fashion, growth in the speed at which these things changed. It was not merely a question for businesses of 'responding' almost instantly to the increasingly volatile 'demand' of customers: they had to anticipate, accentuate and create the volatility, inconstancy and ephemerality of fashions and desires, to stand out against any normalization and any sense of normality. Normality had become a factor of rigidity constraining demand, which could now be stimulated only by the supply of something surprising and unexpected. Any form of rigidity became a shackle to be thrown off.

The fact was that rigidities were inherent in the Fordist mode of production. In that mode, work was broken down into narrowly specialized, unskilled tasks performed on long assembly lines designed for the mass production of standardized products. That meant long lead times to plan and develop new products, given the rigidity of the organization of production and the narrow specialization of the labour force. There was a rigid, quasi-military hierarchy and hosts of supervisory staff to oversee the workers, all of them isolated at their respective work stations, with the synchronization and co-ordination of the fragmented tasks organized and imposed by the overseers. Production targets and the time allotted to each fragmentary task (determined to the hundredth of a second) were further sources of in-built rigidity, with every delay at one work station impacting on the whole of the line.[1] Moreover, there were high levels of stock and warehousing costs and a large number of staff, representing around a quarter of the company's labour force, who were not directly productive.

'Management is so preoccupied with its efforts to establish control over the workers,' observed an American sociologist writing in the 1950s, 'that it loses sight of the presumed purpose of the organization. A casual visitor to the plant might indeed be surprised to learn that its purpose was to get out production. Certainly, if it had been possible to enforce some of the rules described . . . , the result would have been a slowing down of production.'[2]

This obsession with controls did not arise out of the technical imperatives of mass production. On the contrary, as F. W. Taylor had spelled out very explicitly, it arose from the management's fundamental distrust of a labour force regarded as 'naturally' work-shy and stupid. The 'scientific' organization of work was aimed at wringing the highest possible output from the workers by imprisoning them in a system of constraints which removed all scope for initiative. The organization and techniques deployed reflected capital's resolve to dominate labour totally, in order to combat 'indolence', idleness, indiscipline and any inclination to rebel. The factory was the site of a permanent guerrilla war, with the unskilled workers employing enormous ingenuity to conceal sizeable scope for additional productivity (most often around 20 per cent) from the watchful eyes of the supervisory staff. All the skills and creativity of the workers were employed in carving out hidden enclaves of autonomy for themselves.

So long as its aim was to eliminate the human factor by replacing an increasingly rebellious workforce by robots, factory automation remained a source of expensive disappointments. The most famous of these in Europe was the Fiat factory at Cassino, which came on stream in the early eighties. This was to be the most 'advanced' and automated factory in the world. Being a typical product of engineers trained on Taylorist lines, it sought to combine robotization with the centralized monitoring and rigorous programming of sequences and time.

At the same time, in factories they had bought up or were running as 'joint ventures', the Japanese for their part were introducing into the United States methods known as 'lean production' which were going to 'change the world'.[3] For example, when Matsushita bought up Motorola's television plant in Chicago, it proceeded to lay off all the supervisory staff, retaining only the directly productive workers. 'The Americans,' as a Japanese manager explained at the time, 'divide the workforce into those who think and those who work. With us, the workers are also the thinkers, so we need only half the personnel.' In two years, Matsushita doubled the production of TV sets in Chicago and achieved a fiftyfold reduction in the number of final adjustments required.

Kosuke Ikebuchi, senior managing director of the factory which Toyota and General Motors run as a joint venture at Fremont, California, sums up Toyota's philosophy by pointing out that his 2,100 production workers spend eight hours a day on the shopfloor, his engineers only three. As a result, the engineers' main role is to support the workers' ideas, not tell them what to do. Any other attitude, he argues, would be a waste of an enormous resource.[4]

In fact the 'Toyota' or 'Ohno' System (as it is known, after its inventor, T. Ohno) provided the ideal solution to the problem Western industries were now running up against, a problem with which Japanese industrialists had long been familiar. That problem, to use Ohno's words, was: 'what to do to raise productivity when the quantities to be produced do not increase'.[5] However, Ohno's response represented, in a sense, a cultural revolution for Western societies where the history of industrialization is entirely co-terminous with the history of class struggle. One of its essential principles was that a broad measure of worker self-management of the production process is indispensable to achieve maximum flexibility, productivity and speed in both the development of techniques and the adjustment of production to demand. Whereas, for Taylorism, the self-organization, ingenuity and creativity of the workers were to be combated as the source of all dangers of rebellion and disorder, for Toyotism these things were a resource to be developed and exploited. The total and entirely repressive domination of the worker's personality was to be replaced by the total mobilization of that personality. The rigidly fixed techniques imposed on the operatives from above were to be swept away and replaced by '*kaizen*', the continual adjustment and improvement of the manufacturing process by the workers themselves. Only such an absence of formal direction allows the kind of spontaneous and flexible 'productive cooperation' to take place which will yield flexibility in production, optimum time-management and the harmonization of each stage of the manufacturing process with the preceding ones – in a word, '*kan-ban*'.[6]

The workers must understand what they are doing. Indeed, they must (in theory) come to grasp the complete manufacturing process and system as an intelligible whole. They must 'own' that system, control it and feel in command of its workings. They must think about ways of improving and rationalizing product design. They must reflect on possible improvements to procedures and to the overall organization of the system. To this end, they must consult and engage in discussion; they must be able to express themselves and listen; they must be ready to question their own assumptions, to learn, and to develop continually.

The worker, writes Benjamin Coriat, must become simultaneously 'manufacturer, technologist and manager'. As a multi-skilled individual responsible for a range of operations and presiding over a multi-functional, modular set of work 'tools', each worker must 'interface' with the members of his/her own group, and with the groups further up and down the line, to become the collective manager of a common endeavour.

Work done directly on production is now merely one aspect among others of the worker's labour. It is now no longer the most important aspect, but merely the product, continuation and material application of a non-material, intellectual labour of thought, consultation, information exchange, pooling of observation and knowledge, which is performed as much before work as directly in the production context. In short, productive work requires from the workers a 'general social knowledge' which, as the basis of their productivity, enters into the production process as 'a direct force of production'. We shall come back at a later stage to this 'general intellect', which is tending in the eyes of most Marxists to become the dominant form of labour power in an economy itself dominated by non-material activities.[7]

This at least is the ideal model of the post-Fordist enterprise. In that enterprise, the paradigm of organization is replaced by that of the network of interconnected flows, co-ordinated at their nodes by self-organized collectives, none of which occupies a central position. In place of a centrally hetero-organized system (like the Fordist model), we have an acentric self-organizing one, comparable to a nervous system – a model which the interconnected networks attempt to imitate. The question now arises whether this conception opens up unprecedented scope for workers' power, and whether it heralds a possible liberation both *within* work and *from* work. Or does it, rather, carry the subjugation of workers to new heights, forcing them to take on both the function of management and the 'competitive imperative', to put the interests of the company before everything else, including their health and even their lives?[8] Does it represent the introduction of a new feudalism into social relations of production – the worker becoming the 'proud vassal' of a company whose interests he/she is enjoined to identify totally with his/her own – or does it bear within it the seeds of a total seizure of power by the workers, who will come to see capitalist ownership of the company as an obsolete, parasitic structure?[9]

The answer to these questions is largely dependent on the historical, political and economic context in which the post-Fordist principles are applied, in full or in part. As Benjamin Coriat notes:

the problem is that the epoch-making transition we are living through is happening in the worst possible conditions. The crisis and breakdown of Fordism and its specific compromises are – even today – taking place in conditions in which the balance of forces is disastrous for employees and their representatives. And this gives companies very little incentive to embark upon innovative processes. It is so much simpler merely to 'firm up' what one is already doing. And yet . . .'[10]

And yet, everywhere the Fordist/Taylorist method has been more or less completely left behind, post-Fordism presents itself *both* as the heralding of a *possible* reappropriation of work by the workers and as the regression towards a total subjugation and quasi-vassaldom of the very person of the worker. Both aspects are always present. The emancipatory character of post-Fordism has only won out very fleetingly in the rare cases where the 'involvement' demanded of the workers could be negotiated by a trade union which had not yet been weakened by an 'historic defeat'.[11]

UDDEVALLA

The most interesting of these cases is that of the Uddevalla Volvo factory. Instrumental in the conception and creation of that factory was a trade union which had the aim of ridding industry of Taylorism and giving workers genuine control of the organization of work, including the distribution of tasks and time management. The trade union (Metall) had laid down four demands to be met by the team of academics from Gothenburg responsible for designing an assembly unit with optimally attractive working conditions:

1 Work had to be done at 'fixed work bays'.
2 There had to be no set pace of work, which meant that workers had to be able to work and move at their own speed, not at one imposed by a line advancing automatically at regular, centrally programmed speeds (as was still the case at Kalmar).
3 'Work cycles' had to be at least 20 minutes long (as against 4 minutes at Kalmar and 2 minutes in German factories), which

meant that each worker was responsible for a varied and complex set of operations on each vehicle. Work was thereby to become much less repetitive and monotonous.

4 'Indirect labour', usually assigned to a foreman or technician, was to be integrated into the workers' tasks. Such indirect labour comprised, among other things, logistics, the structuring and preparation of parts and equipment, quality control, final checks and adjustments, the training of new employees, group leadership, etc.

The aim was to '*get the workers to think about their own work*' and to '*pose questions also about the design of the product and the machinery*'.[12] That aim was of particular importance to a trade union intending to have a say in production decisions and to subordinate these, eventually, to its own ideas on economic priorities and the model of consumption.[13]

Uddevalla was organized into working groups nine-strong, with eight assembly workers and one person responsible for liaising with the stores. Depending on the wishes and aptitudes of its members, a group could assemble a quarter, a half, three-quarters or the whole of a vehicle (this last requiring ten hours in all). A bonus system provided an incentive for the workers to learn to assemble a complete car. Each of the eight members of the team had to master at least one-quarter (i.e. two-eighths) of the range of operations in order to be able to form a team with another member and be interchangeable with him/her, thus varying the work even more. The group also had to be able to function if, for some reason, one or two of its members were absent.

The organization of the workshop expressly allowed for margins of 'voluntary flexibility' or, in other words, for each member of a group to take days off at times pre-arranged with his/her fellow team members. It also allowed for the possibility of varying the pace of work over a day or a week, or from one week to another, the norm to be met being set on a monthly basis. Each group had its 'ombudsman', a position held in turn by all those members who had chosen to take the relevant additional training course. The members of each group also took it in turns to wash the team members' overalls in the machine provided for that purpose in the changing rooms.

In this way, the relation to work and to the product was profoundly transformed and the three conditions for transcending the alienation of labour were on the way to being *partly* met.[14] These three conditions are:[15]

1   self-organization of work by the workers themselves, who thus become the active subjects of their productive co-operation;
2   work and a mode of co-operation experienced as fulfilling by all and developing faculties and skills which each person can deploy, autonomously, in his/her free time;
3   the materialization of work in a product which is recognizable by the workers as the meaning and goal of their own activity.

It was mainly with regard to this last point that an insurmountable barrier persisted: production decisions specifying what was to be produced remained solely in the hands of the representatives of capital. The quality of that product depended to an unprecedented degree on the involvement of the collective of workers, but that involvement, though conditional and negotiated, continued to be in the service of production decisions which neither the workers themselves nor citizens/users had been able to debate. The goal of their work was imposed on them and its meaning hidden from them, that goal and that meaning being, in the last analysis, the optimum valorization of capital. It is, therefore, somewhat hasty to assert, as Philippe Zariffian does, that the work of post-Fordist workers takes on its full meaning as a result of the fact that each worker 'can grasp the antecedent context of his actions and, starting from that context,' can 'recognize' the 'raison d'être' of the 'production system . . . in the service relation to users or customers'.[16] In fact, taking the best possible view of it, that system is serving individual users of commodities designed for individual use by people who can pay for them. This is, as it happens, an arrangement which excludes the development of public transport systems and, more generally, the non-commodity satisfaction of collective needs by collective means.

Now, the *political stakes* of the antagonism between capital and living labour lie at the level of production decisions – at the level where the content of needs and the ways of satisfying them are being decided. What is at stake politically is, in the last analysis, the *power* to decide the destination and social use of production – that is to say, the mode of consumption for which it is intended and the social relations determined by that mode of consumption.[17]

The Uddevalla factory, which was designed and built between 1984 and 1988 and brought into service in 1989 in a period of full employment in which Volvo, out of a concern for productivity and quality, were still trying to attract and bed in a young, well-trained, highly motivated workforce, was closed for good in 1993. The economic situation had in the interim turned around and the balance of social forces had been reversed: the Swedish unemployment rate had risen from 1.8 per cent in 1990 to 7 per cent in 1992 and to over 10 per cent by 1994. Staff turnover, which had been above 30 per cent in the 1960s, was down to 11.5 per cent in 1990 and around 5 per cent in 1993. It was no longer necessary to offer the labour force attractive working conditions to retain them and ensure their 'involvement'. Although productivity at Uddevalla was higher than at Kalmar and much higher than in the corporation's traditional factories, and although the quality of the products was better than anything that was found in the other factories, it was that model factory, in the van of progress, which the management chose to close (Kalmar was shut down the following year). Jean-Pierre Durand offers a twofold explanation for this decision:

With repetitive tasks having been done away with at Uddevalla, the factory could not develop towards more thoroughgoing automation. At the Ghent factory, by contrast, as in all those organized on Japano-American 'lean production' lines (in Germany, Great Britain and France), repetitive tasks (in basic cycles of 1.8 to 1.9 minutes) still exist, making progress possible at a later date to virtually full-scale robotization.

As a result of abolishing the centrally programmed, set-speed assembly-line, the smooth functioning of the Uddevalla factory depended, far more than any other, on the involvement and commitment of its workforce. They were no longer subject to any hierarchical supervision or power, nor to any of the constraints imposed on workers in other factories which subjected them to systems with pre-programmed parameters. In short, workers' power over production seemed in the end to have been pointlessly and dangerously extended . . . Globalization and unemployment enabled capital to regain undivided power once more. This was precisely the function they were meant to perform.[18]

SUBJECTION

The 'problem', as Coriat put it, is that the liberatory potential of post-Taylorism could only be realized by moving beyond capitalist social relations. Capital applies certain post-Taylorist principles where it can be sure it has forearmed itself against the autonomous use by workers of the limited power conceded to them. In Japan, the United States and Europe, the companies which have adopted the principles of lean production – or some of them – take on only young, carefully pre-selected workers with no trade-union past, and, particularly in Great Britain, force them in their contracts of employment to give an undertaking, on pain of dismissal, never to strike or join any union other than the company's own. In a word, they employ workers only when stripped of their class identity, of their place in and membership of the wider society.

In exchange, they offer their young workers an identity derived from the 'corporate culture', the symbolism of which is developed by each firm at a number of different levels: the company's own brand of vocational training; a specific in-house vocabulary and style of behaviour; a distinctive code of dress, to some degree approaching the company uniform favoured in Japan.

In a disintegrating society, in which the quest for identity and the pursuit of social integration are continually being frustrated, the 'corporate culture' and 'corporate loyalty' inculcated by the firm offer the young workers a substitute for membership of the wider society, a refuge from the sense of insecurity. The firm offers them the kind of security monastic orders, sects and work communities provide. It asks them to give up everything – to give up any other form of allegiance, their personal interests and even their personal life – in order to *give themselves*, body and soul, to the company which, in exchange, will provide them with an identity, a place, a personality and a job they can be proud of. They become members of a 'big family.' The relationship to the company and to the corporate work collective becomes the only social bond; it absorbs all the workers' energy and mobilizes their whole person, thus storing up the danger for them of a *total loss of self-worth* if they were one day no longer to deserve the confidence of the firm and the consideration of their fellow team-members, both of which are earned by indefinitely improving their performance.

Hence, the *virtual* emancipation of post-Fordist workers *within their work* is accompanied by reinforced social control. That control, as indeed Coriat remarks, takes the particular form of 'ostracism', of the subjection of individuals to the conformist, totalitarian pressure of the group. The conception of the 'integrated factory', the integrative company, clearly bears the stamp of its Japanese origin by the quasi-feudal way the company is represented as a community of work and allegiance in which there cannot, and must not, be any social antagonisms or conflicts of interest. The company is supposed to function in the common interest and for the common good of all its members. There can be no 'negotiation': all problems are to be settled consensually on the basis of attentive examination by all concerned.

There is a clear regression here by comparison with Fordism: Toyotism replaces modern social relations with pre-modern ones. Fordism was in fact modern in so far as it recognized the specificity of, and antagonism between, the respective interests of living labour and capital. The relationship between the company and the workers was in essence a conflictual one and required of the parties concerned *negotiated compromises* which are continually undergoing review. Workers did not *belong* to the company. They owed it only the work clearly laid down in their contracts of employment, at set hours and on specified terms and conditions. They owed it to the company to *lend themselves* to the accomplishment of tasks which could be effected without their committing themselves to the particular ends concerned. The achievement of those ends was guaranteed by predefined operational procedures, and these were designed to leave the outcome of the operations largely independent of the intentions, personalities and goodwill of the operators. That outcome was not to be ascribed to them personally. It did not require their subjective involvement, or at most it required it only incidentally. As subjects, their sense of belonging to themselves – to their own trade unions, their class, their society – was stronger than their sense of belonging to the company. The rights inherent in their social and political citizenship were of greater consequence than their employer's rights to dispose of their labour, their abilities, their persons. They retained a substantial part of their energies for themselves, that part being effectively withdrawn from productive instrumentalization – from exploitation. They accepted their alienation conditionally, in a sphere circumscribed by collective action and negotiation and by labour law. The conflictual dynamics of Fordist relations of production tended towards ever greater limitation of the space-time available to capital for exploiting labour and of the scope of that exploitation. It is this dynamic which was first halted, then reversed, in post-Fordism.

In the name of the need to compete, post-Fordism gradually won back the ground businesses had had to yield during the Fordist period. It drove increasingly large holes into labour law and the provisions of collective bargaining agreements, making it a principle that employees' allegiance to the company must outweigh their allegiance to their class or society, and that the company's rights over 'its' workers must outweigh the rights conferred by social and economic citizenship. It demanded unconditional and personal *devotion* to the company's goals and turned the whole person – linguistic abilities, learning, predictive and analytic skills – into an instrument serving those goals. The company first bought 'the person and their commitment' and only then did it develop their 'capacity for abstract labour'.[19] It shaped and conditioned that person and 'narrowed their horizon to that of the factory. The subjectivity which unfolds here is the opposite of a free subjectivity, set against the 'world of things,' for . . . the subject's lifeworld is circumscribed by the company's system of ends and values . . . No physical or psychical space remains which is not occupied by company logic.'[20]

We have in some ways left behind the realm of abstract labour, which, being performed as an impersonal task independent of the employee's and the employer's personality, put an end, in Marx's view, to pre-capitalist relations of personal submission, and we have returned to personalized 'service', which is impossible to describe in formal terms and difficult to embody in a contract. This re-establishes, as Paul Virno puts it, the relation of worker to employer on the basis of 'universal personal dependence in a dual sense: on the one hand, one is dependent on a particular person, not on rules endowed with an anonymous power of coercion; on the other, it is the whole person, the ability to think and act – in short, each person's "species being" – which is subjugated'. The result is 'universally subservient labour', 'total subjection. No one is quite so poor as the person who sees his relations to others or his language abilities reduced to the status of paid work.'[21]

This kind of analysis inevitably makes one wonder whether this total subjugation of the whole person does not stand in flagrant contradiction to the initiative, creativity and autonomy with which workers are supposed to commit their whole selves to their group work. Capital calls on them to consult and reflect, to plan and discuss what they do, to be the autonomous subjects of production, but it enjoins them also to confine their autonomy within pre-set limits and direct it towards preordained aims. Maurizio Lazzarato sums up this contradiction very well: '"Be active subjects!" is the new command echoing through Western societies today . . . You must express yourself, speak, communicate, co-operate . . . [But] the communicative relationship is completely predetermined in both content and form.' It is, more precisely, made a function of, an instrument in the service of, a technical system which requires coded information to circulate at a particular velocity. 'The subject,' observes Lazzarato, 'is a mere coding and decoding station . . . The communicative relation has to eliminate the features which actually constitute [the subject's] specificity.'[22]

AUTONOMY AND THE SALE OF SELF

The contradiction we run up against here is precisely the one I termed 'autonomy within heteronomy', when I observed that labour, in its struggles, has always fought over the nature of the limitations capital imposes on the autonomy of living labour.[23] Theoretically, when autonomy increases, the rejection of heteronomy should become more radical. The autonomy the company requires of the worker should tend to assert itself *independently of the company's need for it* and should increase in all areas. The worker who is autonomous at work should, sooner or later, refuse to be reduced to a predetermined productive function. In the end, the worker should question every external control over the character, organization and goal of work, including the economic and political decisions which condition it. The supporters of workers' control, of worker 'self-management', started out from a hypothesis which was in their eyes self-evidently true: once demands for autonomy and power have been won in the workplace, there will be no way to limit them generally.

I argued this position myself in the 1960s.[24] I find it again today in a radicalized and highly schematic form in the writings of most theorists of 'mass intellectuality'. Yet, there is one difference between us since, in their view, total autonomy and emancipation are no longer *demands which tend to arise*, but a present reality. In their view, 'work is immediately something free and constructive.'[25] 'Capital becomes merely an apparatus of capture, a phantasm, an idol.'[26] 'Mass intellectuality' – which comprises the men and women who, whether in work or not, possess those most *common* skills and capacities which are put to work by the post-Fordist production process (the capacity to interpret, communicate, imagine, anticipate, etc.) – is said to be ready to constitute itself as an alternative power, since 'the production process of subjectivity, that is to say the production process *per se* [!], forms itself "outside" the relation to capital and "within" processes constitutive of mass intellectuality or, in other words, in the subjectivization of labour.'[27] The social process of production is said to generate the collective subject of an alternative power (in other words, the subject of the proletarian communist revolution) as a result of the fact that, as P. Zariffian has it, '[thanks to *kan-ban*], each individual can grasp the overall workings of the production system, the end-goal of that production . . . and the network of interactions into which each action fits . . . as a totality constitutive of those interactions.'[28] 'The working individual liberates himself', he 'is free', since he 'does not submit to the constraints of an external order but follows out the internal determination which lays down the possibilities of, and reasons for, productive action.'[29]

Underlying these theoreticist ravings, which have not been without their influence on the broader Marxist movement, we always find the implicit assumption that autonomy in work generates, in and of itself, the workers' capacity to abolish any limit or obstacle to the exercise of their autonomy. Now, this is obviously not the case. Autonomy in work is of little significance when it is not carried into the cultural, moral and political spheres; and cultural, moral and political autonomy does not arise from productive co-operation itself but from activism, and from the culture of resistance, rebellion, fraternity, free debate, radical questioning and dissidence which that activism produces.

In their haste to come up with an inherently revolutionary subject engendered by the production process, these authors resort to a kind of systemist Spinozism which evades the most difficult task, namely that of creating the cultural and political mediations through which the challenge to the mode and goals of production will emerge. In so doing, they merely throw into sharper relief the questions they sidestep. For example, is the system of production designed, managed and organized so as to ensure the greatest possible autonomy of workers both in their work and in their lives outside their work? To what – and to whose – ends are the products of their labours put? Where do the needs come from which their products are supposed to meet? Who lays down how these needs and desires are to be met and, as a consequence, prescribes the prevailing model of consumption and civilization? And, most importantly, what are the relations between the *actual* participants in the production process and the *potential* or peripheral participants in that process – that is to say, the unemployed, the temporary or casual workers, freelancers and self-employed outworkers?

Capital has its answers to all these questions and, as we shall see, it is precisely by shielding these from debate or challenge, by presenting them as 'natural laws', that it has managed to control the autonomy of workers who, in their work, stand outside its command. In other words, *lean production itself produces the social and cultural conditions which enable capital to control the autonomy of living labour.*

Paolo Virno brings out one important aspect of this problem when he writes:

> It is no longer labour time, but science, information, knowledge in general and linguistic communication which now figure as the 'central pillar' sustaining production and wealth . . . In the age of the general intellect, the whole salaried labour force has the permanent status of a 'reserve army.' And this is so even when they are subject to the most punishing shift work schedules.[30]

This is the case because the skills and capacities deployed in work are 'the most commonly available' – are 'mass intellectuality' – so that *anyone, male or female, is both potentially in work and potentially redundant.* 'Mass intellectuality,' writes Virno, denotes 'a quality and distinguishing mark of the entire labour force of the post-Fordist era, in which information and communication play a key role in every facet of the production process; *in short, in the era in which language itself has been put to work, in which it has become wage labour.*'[31]

Now, when imaginative and co-operative relational and communicational capacities become part of labour power, those capacities, which imply the autonomy of the subject, cannot of their essence be produced to order: they will exist and be deployed not *to order,* but on the subject's initiative. Capital's domination cannot, there-fore, be exerted *directly* over living labour by hierarchical constraints. That control can only be exerted in indirect ways: it has to shift upstream from the factory and take the form of a conditioning which leads the subject to *accept* or *choose* precisely what can no longer be *imposed*. The factory, the workplace, then cease to be the main arena of the central conflict. The battle lines of that conflict will be every-where information, language, modes of life, tastes and fashions are produced and shaped by the forces of capital, commerce, the state and the media; in other words, everywhere the subjectivity and 'identity' of individuals, their values and their images of themselves and the world, are being continually structured, manufactured and shaped. I shall come back to this point at the end of this book in connection with what Alain Touraine terms 'programmed society'. The battle lines of the conflict are drawn up everywhere and the radicalization of that conflict in the area of culture (of education, training, cities, leisure and lifestyle) is the precondition for its radi-calization in the area of work. Consequently, there can be no effec-tive trade unionism which remains exclusively focused on the workplace and on defending that section of the workforce which is in stable employment.

By the instability, volatility, flexibility, ephemerality and insub-stantiality it produces in all fields, material and immaterial, post-Fordism produces the ideological and cultural conditions required for it to dominate its 'involved' workers. In fact, the subjugation by capital of workers whom capital simultaneously enjoins to be autonomous subjects, creative in their labours, has always existed. There have always been activities and occupations in which workers had to be both autonomous and totally involved in their tasks and accept that the nature, goal and meaning of that task were imposed upon them. The order to be 'active subjects', but to be so in the service of an Other whose rights you will never contest, is in fact the accepted lot of all those creative individuals *with a real, but limited, subjugated sovereignty*, the jobbing producers of ideas, fantasies and messages. This includes journalists, propagandists, advertising copy-writers and artists, 'public relations' specialists, and researchers in death-dealing civil or military industries – in a word, all who *give wholly of their persons* in the service of activities which are gratifying *in themselves*, but by way of which they become the venal and eager instruments of an alien will: in which they *sell themselves*. For what they get paid for is not an objectivized product which could be detached from their persons, but the deployment of their creative skills, of their 'talents' for purposes dictated by their employer or client. Sovereignly free within limits imposed by someone else; free to achieve the aims of a master, but free for that only. Now, selling oneself, and particularly, selling 'the whole of oneself', including what is most common to human beings – 'in a word, in one's species being' – is not simply, as Virno believes, the behaviour of a 'servant': it is the very essence of prostitution. For prostitution is not simply 'the sale of one's body', since body and sexuality are not separable from the whole person, and their sale is always a *sale of self*. Lazzarato's argument that 'the involvement of the subject under capitalist command does not engage the deep layers of the personality and social being' is the classic alibi of those who sell and prostitute themselves while claiming that this does not affect their integrity. That integrity is always at stake, whether one prostitutes one's body, one's intelligence, one's talent or any other resource which is *not detachable* from the subject deploying it.[32]

The sale of self reaches its height among freelance providers of professional services who are both their own fixed capital, its valorization by labour, the commodity sold on the market and the promoters, by a carefully elaborated commercial strategy, of that commodity. They regard themselves as 'working commodities' and thus take to its logical conclusions the ideology of the 'Japanese industrialists of the post-Fordist era for whom being a working commodity is the only possible way of being "human," a conception which leads inevitably to conformism'.[33] The ideology which makes 'knowing how to sell oneself' the greatest virtue plays a decisive role here and contributes to the development of that 'personality market' C. Wright Mills described as long ago as the early 1950s.[34] Henceforth, the personality is an integral part of labour power. In the past, this was the case only for personal servants and those service-sector workers who were in direct contact with their clients. In the post-Fordist enterprise, technical knowledge and professional skills are only of value when combined with a particular *state of mind*, an unlimited openness to adjustment, change, the unforeseen; in short, that willing disposition which in English is termed 'eagerness'. It is the applicants' personalities, their attitudes to work that will decide in the first instance whether or not they are employed.

WORK WHICH IS ABOLISHING WORK

The ideology of selling oneself clearly could not prevail if post-Fordism did not of itself create the macro-social conditions which both mask the liberatory potentialities of technical change and enable that change to become an instrument of reinforced domination. These macro-social effects, on the structure and volume of employment in particular, are spelled out with rare frankness in an interview given by Peter Haase, the head of training at Volkswagen.[35]

Haase first explains that 'transferring entrepreneurial skills to the shopfloor' makes it possible 'largely to eliminate the antagonisms between labour and capital . . . If the work teams have great independence to plan, carry out and monitor processes, material flows, staffing and skills . . . then you have a large enterprise made up of independent small entrepreneurs, and that constitutes a cultural revolution.'

But that 'revolution', which is entirely consonant with the Toyota system, clearly presupposes that the workers have the capacity to analyse, predict, communicate and express themselves, capacities which the 'mass intellectuality' theorists regard as belonging to the 'general intellect'. Ideal apprentices, says Haase, must have command of their native language, written and spoken, and should be capable, by their knowledge of a foreign language, of blending into a foreign culture.

'What about those who aren't good at languages and don't have technical or scientific qualifications?'

'They are pushed to the fringes of the labour market,' replies Haase. 'That is becoming an enormous problem.'

That problem, Haase points out, has in part to do with the fact that 'the time it takes for knowledge to lose half its value is growing shorter and shorter. With computer hardware and software, the time scale is now 12–24 months. Most people are trying to respond to this situation by atomizing knowledge. But atomized knowledge then has to be continually put back together again.'

'The only solution for adolescents without qualifications is to learn a trade, then?'

'In the craft sector too, only the best get jobs. After industry has cherry-picked the year's school-leavers, the craft sector takes the best of the remainder. The rest are thrown on the scrap heap . . . What are we to do when there isn't enough work for everyone? Basically, it would be best if young people could work a 40- or 50-hour week at the beginning of their careers. If they are allowed to work only 20 hours, they develop a very bad attitude to work.'

It could hardly be more clearly stated that the workers taken on by the big companies are a small 'elite', not because they have higher levels of skill, but because they have been chosen from a mass of equally able individuals in such a way as to perpetuate the work ethic in an economic context in which work is objectively losing its 'centrality': the economy has less and less need of it. The passion for, devotion to, and identification with work would be diminishing if everyone were able to work less and less. It is economically more advantageous to concentrate the small amount of necessary work in the hands of a few, who will be imbued with the sense of being a deservedly privileged elite by virtue of the eagerness which distinguishes them from the 'losers'. Technically, there is really nothing to prevent the firm from sharing out the work between a larger number of people who would work only 20 hours a week. But then those people would not have the 'correct' attitude to work which consists in regarding themselves as small entrepreneurs turning their knowledge capital to good effect.

So, the firm 'largely . . . eliminate[s] the antagonisms between capital and labour' for the stable core of its elite workers and shifts those antagonisms outside its field of vision, to the peripheral, insecure or unemployed workers. Post-Fordism produces its elite by producing unemployment; the latter is the precondition for the former. The 'social utility' of that elite cannot, for that reason, be assessed solely from the angle of the use-value of its production or the 'service rendered to users'. Its members can no longer believe themselves useful in a general way, since *they produce wealth and unemployment in the self-same act*. The greater their productivity and eagerness for work, the greater also will be unemployment, poverty, inequality, social marginalization and the rate of profit. The more they identify with work and with their company's successes, the more they contribute to producing and reproducing the conditions of their own subjection, to intensifying the competition between firms, and hence to making the battle for productivity the more lethal, the threat to everyone's employment – including their own – the more menacing, and the domination of capital over workers and society the more irresistible.

I recall these obvious points for all those who enthuse over the autonomy, involvement and identification with work encouraged by post-Fordism without warning that the effect and function of that work is drastically to reduce the volume of employment, drastically to reduce the volume of wages distributed, and to raise the rate of exploitation to previously unattained heights. Post-Fordist industry is the spearhead of a thoroughgoing transformation which is abolishing work, abolishing the wage relation and tending to reduce the proportion of the working population who carry out the whole of material production to 2 per cent. It is crazy to present a form of work which ensures that there is less and less work and wages for everyone as the essential source of autonomy, identity and fulfilment *for all*.

I am not saying, however, that post-Fordist workers cannot or ought not to identify with what they do. I am saying that what they do cannot and should not be reduced solely to the immediately productive work they accomplish, irrespective of the consequences and mediate effects which it engenders in the social environment. I say, therefore, that they must identify with *everything* they do, that they must make their work their own and assume responsibility for it as subjects, not excluding from this the consequences it produces in the social field. I say that they ought to be the subjects of – and also the actors in – the abolition of work, the abolition of employment, the abolition of wage labour, instead of abandoning all these macro-economic and macro-social dimensions of their productive activity to market forces and capital. They ought, therefore, to make the redistribution of work, the diminution of its intensity, the reduction of working hours, the self-management of the hours and pace of work, and the guarantee of purchasing power demands inherent in the meaning of their work. And they ought to do so not solely at company or sub-sector level, but at the level of the whole society and the economic space of which it is a part. The appropriation of work to the point of incorporating its consequences and indirect effects calls for a trade-union policy and a political trade unionism.

METAMORPHOSES OF WAGE LABOUR

By substituting the paradigm of the acentric, self-organized network for that of the centred, hierarchical organization, post-Fordism has, in the end, changed the nature of the wage relation much more than the nature of work. The focus in the Toyota system on 'putting to work what is most specifically human' most often masks the reintroduction of massive doses of Taylorism in the very heart of the Japanese system and its Western adaptations. Above all, it leaves out of account the transformations which post-Fordist business brings about in its social environment, and in society as a whole.

It has to be kept in mind that, at Toyota itself, the company organized on Ohno's principles is simply the final assembly plant employing only 10–15 per cent of the labour force involved in manufacturing the complete product. That assembly plant is the tip of a pyramid (*keiretsu*) which rests on a total of 45,000 subcontracting companies that are increasingly Taylorized as one moves down towards the base. There are 171 'first-rank' subcontractors providing complete sub-assemblies, developed in collaboration with the parent company; 5,000 second-rank subcontractors providing components for the first-rank companies; and 40,000 third-rank subcontractors providing parts for the others. As one moves away from the apex of the pyramid, the technical level of the companies, the skill levels required and the wages paid all fall. In the first-rank subcontractors, which are computerized, robotized and employ between 100 and 500 persons, wages are 25 per cent lower than what is paid in the parent company. In the subcontractors with fewer than 100 employees, wages are 45 per cent lower, and often even lower than that for insecure, irregular work, paid on piece rates.

The parent company effectively 'farms out' all the specialized tasks which other companies can take on equally well and more economically. The state of dependency in which it keeps its subcontractors allows it to impose continual price reductions on them and pass on fluctuations in demand. For the labour forces of the subcontractors, the effect of those fluctuations is felt in the 'flexibility' of hours and staffing levels. Alain Lebaube summed the situation up well:

> Whilst the company refocuses on its core activity and tends to upgrade the jobs of its personnel, it shifts the most painful constraints, which often take the form of Taylorized working conditions, on to a network of subcontractors. The 'fragmented' enterprise hypocritically closes its eyes to the social consequences of this division, and to the implications of the specifications it imposes on its suppliers.[36]

The labour force is thus split into two major categories: a central core made up of permanent and full-time employees, who are occupationally versatile and mobile, and, around that core, a sizeable mass of peripheral workers, including a substantial proportion of insecure and temporary workers with variable hours and wages. To these peripheral employees must be added an increasingly significant proportion of 'outworkers', that is to say, of supposedly 'self-employed' operatives, paid on a sessional basis or on piece work, whose workload varies according to the needs of the moment. These 'freelancers' are not covered by labour law, have no social insurance and are exposed to all the commercial and economic risks which the company offloads on to them.

In 1986, Wolfgang Lecher predicted that the proportion of stable, full-time jobs would fall to 50 per cent within ten years.[37] According to forecasts made in 1994, stable, full-time employment in Germany will fall to only 30–40 per cent by the year 2003. Great Britain is already below this level. In Britain, 95 per cent of new jobs are insecure, as against 75–80 per cent in France, where 40 per cent are part-time or based on fixed-term contracts.

According to Womack, the Western adaptation of the Toyota system ought to make it possible to manufacture the same volume of products with half as large a workforce, half as much capital, and premises half as large, in half the time. The time required for designing and developing new products ought also to be reduced by half, as should the working hours of the research department.

Three years after Womack's book, the tendency to replace the organizing structure by the acentric management of flows was radicalized by a former MIT professor under the banner of 're-engineering'.[38] This involved extending just-in-time methods to personnel management, reducing permanent staffing levels by at least 40 per cent – and even 80 per cent in the big network firms.

The plan for the reorganization of BankAmerica of California (28,000 employees in 1993) provided a good illustration of this policy. The proposal was to retain only 19 per cent of the permanent employees; the remaining 81 per cent were to become outworkers (some of them teleworking) and be paid according to the number of sessions or hours of work the company needed at the time. In the great majority of cases, their average workload was to be less than 20 hours per week.

Re-engineering extended with traumatic rapidity to all fields of activity. Since 1993, permanent, full-time employees have made up only 10 per cent of the workforces of the 500 largest American companies. In Europe, particularly in Great Britain and France, that particular form of insecure employment known as 'contract work' has developed. These contract workers, found in the public services and elsewhere, do the same work as the regular staff, but have neither the same status, nor the same benefit entitlements, nor the same levels of pay. They are at the beck and call of the employer, who (in the French education system or postal services, for example) guarantees them what is often a derisory minimum of hours per month or per year, without, however, fixing the date and times of their service beforehand: they are informed of these only a day in advance, or even – as in the British 'zero-hours contract' – on the actual day.

Business consultants have evaluated the number of jobs which reorganization – combined with the full utilization of information technologies – will save (that is to say, eliminate) in the various industrial sub-sectors. They have concluded that, out of 90 million jobs in the private sector in the United States, 25 million will disappear.[39] The forecasts are similar for Germany: of the 33 million existing jobs, it will be possible to do away with 9 million by applying more efficient methods which are currently available.[40] According to the Boston Consulting Group, over-staffing in industry is in the region of 30–40 per cent, and in the tertiary sector it is 30–50 per cent. Since the publication of these forecasts in 1993, industry in Germany has increased the number of its robots by 60 per cent and massively reduced its staffing levels. There are almost a million skilled or highly skilled workers and 60,000 engineers and scientists on the unemployment register. The estimate of over-staffing in the tertiary sector did not take into account the coming extension of teleworking, teleshopping and videoconferencing, which will bring about a great reduction of employment levels in shops, estate agents and tourism.

Outsourcing allows capitalism to reinstate the social conditions which prevailed at the beginning of the nineteenth century for a growing proportion of the workforce: the 'contract', temporary, sessional and other insecure workers are comparable to the intermittently employed 'jobbers' who were called on as and when required. The company does not have to pay social insurance contributions, holiday pay, redundancy pay or training allowances for such workers. The logical outcome of the outsourcing process is the abolition of wage-labour itself, a prospect which has been dubbed the post-job society. This would allow the trend towards a 'flexible workforce' to be realized fully, with payment for work becoming freely negotiable between the company and each of its individual contractors. Legal minimum wages and agreed rates of pay would cease to apply. The only thing that would matter would be the law of the market and the relation of forces between the company and the reputedly 'self-employed' person whose work would be purchased on the basis of a commercial agreement. 'What is disappearing today', declares William Bridges, 'is not just a certain number of jobs, [but] the very thing itself: *the job.*' And he adds, 'The post-job worker is going to be far more likely to be hired for a project or for a fixed length of time than a jobholder is today . . . Without the job, time off from work becomes not something taken out of job time but something sandwiched into the interims between assignments or between project contracts.'[41] The company is no longer a workplace or a work collective: it simply calls on providers of services as one might call on a dentist or a plumber when you need one. There is, however, one important difference: the company reserves the right to negotiate and revise the price of each piece of work 'as a function,' says Bridges, 'of the value the supplier can add'.

The wage worker of the Fordist era (the mass worker) is succeeded, then, by two other figures. The first of these, whom we shall look at in the next chapter, is the 'jobber'. The jobber turns insecurity into a way of life in a manner reminiscent of the *vrais sublimes* Poulot wrote of in the middle of the nineteenth century.[42] Refusing either to sell themselves to an employer or to serve capital, these people accept only temporary jobs and gain as much free time for themselves as possible by working just enough to meet their needs. Alongside these 'dissidents' of capitalism stands the only figure to interest the post-job ideologues: the 'freelancer', who is the boss of a one-person enterprise in which he/she is 'self-employed' and for which he/she builds up a 'portfolio' of occasional or regular customers.

The image of 'the self-employed worker' who is 'his/her own boss' is attractive to 40 per cent of young Britons, who say they wish to be paid by their capacities and on merit, rather than by a pre-set scale. Most will quickly discover that they have been duped. The only freelance workers who prosper from this arrangement are the ones who belong to 'the elite of knowledge workers' Rifkin writes of. Those people – consultants, business lawyers, computer and other high-level experts – represent less than 1 per cent of the workforce. For those with no such reputation for possessing the exceptional skills sought by companies, self-employed working will be a source of greater freedom only to the extent that self-employed, unemployed, insecure and temporary workers manage to organize themselves within their pool of employment, set a rate for their services and divide up all the available jobs between themselves as effectively as possible. In the absence of such organization – and only embryonic examples of it exist – the post-job era merely means companies are free to fish out from a well-stocked pool of service-providers of all kinds those who offer the best service at the lowest price.

In the end, the self-employed work at rates and in conditions which employed workers would find unacceptable. According to a survey carried out by the European Commission, more than half of men and one-third of women work 48 hours or more a week throughout the European Community. In France, the figures are 70 per cent and 50 per cent respectively. Self-employed workers, says the report, 'can achieve a decent level of income only by working a great many hours and they are more liable than employed workers to fall below the poverty line'.[43]

The less work there is for everyone, the longer the hours of work tend to become for each individual. Juliet Schor has analysed this paradoxical effect of unemployment in the US case.[44] Unemployment depresses levels of pay and the fall in pay prompts workers to do more hours to make up the shortfall. This in turn accentuates the fall in levels of pay.

The development of so-called self-employment, infinitely 'flexible' in all its parameters, is merely the most visible manifestation of the trend towards the abolition of wage-labour. For this trend is also dominant in the relations between the company and its core workforce. There it takes the form of the individualization and flexibilization of salaries, the division of the large company into 'profit centres' with the employees, as entrepreneurs, responsible for ensuring that profitability is maintained.

Along with abolishing wage-relations, capital is thus attempting to abolish almost all the limits the labour movement has managed to set on exploitation over two centuries of struggle. In replacing collective bargaining by individual negotiation, wage agreements by 'flexible' individualized pay rates, and the wage relation by a commercial relation, capital is substituting for the old constraints, imposed on human beings by the machines they had to serve, new ones 'irresistibly' (because anonymously) imposed by impersonal market 'laws' on dispersed and competing individuals.

The individualization of pay rates, together with the transformation of employees into sessional or self-employed workers, is tending to abolish not only wage-labour but abstract labour itself. Those performing work are no longer treated as members of a group or profession defined by their public status, but as particular providers of particular services in particular conditions. They no longer provide *abstract labour, labour in general, work dissociable from their person* and marking them out as social individuals in general, useful in a general way. Their status is no longer governed by the labour law which meant that the worker belonged first to society and only secondarily to the company. The customers or companies for which they provide their services can treat them unequally, depending on whether or not they like a service worker's attitude or personality, and can pick them on subjective grounds.

In this way, wage-labour is losing the emancipatory function of freeing workers from the relations of subjection which prevailed in traditional society – where social relations were fundamentally inegalitarian and personalized: 'Work was not supplied in that society as *labour*, but as a "service" (*servicium, obsequium*)' owed to the master, whereas in 'modern society, which we then define as "work-based society" . . . exchanges take place mainly on the basis of social relations which are, in principle, of an egalitarian and impersonal type'.[45]

GENERALIZED INSECURITY

We are leaving work-based society behind without replacing it by any other form. *Each* of us is aware, emotionally and intellectually, that we are potentially unemployed, potentially under-employed, potentially insecure or temporary workers, potential 'part-timers'. But what *each* of us knows *individually* has yet to become – and is prevented from becoming – a *common* awareness of our *common* condition: that is to say, an awareness, publicly formulated and accepted, of the fact that the central figure of our society – and the 'normal' condition within that society – is no longer (or is tending no longer to be) that of the 'worker' – nor *a fortiori* that of the blue-collar worker, the white-collar worker, the wage-earner. It is becoming, rather, the figure of the insecure worker, who at times 'works' and at times does not 'work', practises many different trades without any of them actually being a trade, has no identifiable profession or, rather, whose profession it is to have no profession, and cannot therefore identify with his/her work, but regards as his/her 'true' activity the one he/she devotes himself to in the gaps between his/her paid 'work'. It is this insecure worker that is potentially the central figure of our own world; it is this figure which must be *civilized* and *recognized* so that, rather than being a condition one reluctantly bears, this pattern of working can become a mode of life one chooses, a mode that is desirable, one that is regulated and valued by society, a source of new culture, freedoms and sociality, establishing the right of all to choose the discontinuities in their working lives without experiencing a discontinuity in their income.

All the established powers are opposed to this recognition and what it entails. For the unfettered power capital has assumed over labour, society and everyone's lives depends precisely on 'work' – not the work you do, but the work you are made to do – retaining its centrality in everyone's lives and minds, even when it has to a massive extent been eliminated, 'saved' and abolished at all levels of production across the whole of society and throughout the world. Even when post-Fordism, the networked interaction of fractal factories and the 'immaterial' economy are based on a wealth production which is increasingly disconnected from work and an accumulation of profit increasingly disconnected from any production, each person's right to an adequate income, to full citizenship – indeed his/her very right to have rights – is still made to depend on his/her accomplishment of some measurable, classifiable, saleable 'work'. The result is that everyone, unemployed and potentially insecure workers alike, is urged to fight for a share of the 'work' capital is abolishing all around him/her; and every march and every banner declaring 'We want work' proclaims the victory of capital over a subjugated humanity of workers who can no longer be workers, but are denied a chance to be anything else.

This is the nub of the problem, then, and the nub of the conflict: the aim must be to disconnect from 'work' the right to have rights, chief among these being the right to what is produced and producible without work, or at least with increasingly less work. It has to be recognized that neither the right to an income, nor full citizenship, nor everyone's sense of identity and self-fulfilment can any longer be centred on and depend upon occupying a job. And society has to be changed to take account of this.

But this central problem will only be confronted, and the struggle taken up, if 'work' – the work you are given to do – loses its centrality in everyone's minds, thinking and imagination. And this is precisely what all the established powers and dominant forces are working to prevent, with the aid of experts and ideologues who deny that 'work' is being eliminated with increasing rapidity. The place of work in everyone's imagination and self-image and in his/her vision of a possible future is the central issue in a profoundly political conflict, a struggle for power. Any transformation of society, however ripe the conditions may be for it, requires the capacity to think differently, or quite simply to formulate what everyone is actually feeling. It is this question we shall turn to first in the following pages.

3
The Lost Magic of Work

We are living through the extinction of a specific mode of social belonging and a specific type of society, the society Michel Aglietta has termed 'wage-based' and Hannah Arendt 'work-based' (*Arbeitsgesellschaft*). The 'work' which gave one membership of that society is clearly not work in the anthropological or philosophical sense. It is not the work of the peasant ploughing his field, the craftsman fashioning his piece, the writer crafting his text or the musician working at his instrument. The work which is disappearing is 'abstract labour', labour that is measurable, quantifiable and detachable from the person who 'provides' it; work which can be bought and sold in the 'labour market'. It is, in short, the monetarily exchangeable work or commodity labour which was invented and forcibly imposed by manufacturing capitalism from the end of the eighteenth century onwards.[1]

Even in the heyday of wage-based society, that work was never a source of 'social cohesion' or integration, whatever we might have come to believe from its retrospective idealization. The 'social bond' it established between individuals was abstract and weak, though it did, admittedly, *insert* people into the process of social labour, into social relations of production, as functionally specialized cogs in an immense machine.

That work, which was socially determined, acknowledged, legitimated, enshrined in law and defined by certified skills paid for at set rates, met the objective, functional demands of the economic machine. It gave everyone a sense of usefulness, irrespective of his/her intentions. Everyone felt useful in an objective, impersonal, anonymous way, and was recognized as such through the wages received and the accompanying social entitlements. Those entitlements were not attached to the *person* of the wage-earner, but to the function the job fulfilled in the social process of production, that function being in itself immaterial. '*Never mind what work you do, what counts is having a job.*' This was the essential ideological message of the wage-based society. Don't concern yourself too much with what you do, what counts is the pay at the end of the week. It was against this ideology of commodity labour, with neither intrinsic dignity, interest nor meaning, against this constraining, oppressive work, which merely gave access to increasingly lavish consumption, that the workers in the factories, offices and services of Taylorized Fordism mounted increasingly fierce resistance.

As for social integration and cohesion in all this, even at its height, wage-based society was torn and 'fractured' by class divisions and antagonisms. The workers were not integrated into society, but into their class, their trade union, their working community, and it was from their struggles to transform their work, lives and society that they derived their 'identity', dignity, culture and cohesion. And it was against their cohesion, 'identity' and class organization that what is known as 'business' found the absolute, unanswerable weapon: the evanescence of work; its conversion into an individualized, discontinuous activity; its abolition on a massive scale – insecurity of employment for all.

'Fear and tremble.' The ideological message has changed. Where once it was, 'Never mind what work you do, so long as you get paid at the end of the week', it is now, 'Never mind what you're paid, so long as you have a job.' In other words, be prepared to make any and every concession, to suffer humiliation or subjugation, to face competition and betrayal to get or keep a job, since 'those who lose their jobs lose everything'. If this is not the general feeling in society, it is at least the message of the dominant social discourse. It is a message which extols the centrality of work, presents it as a rare commodity, as something one does or does not *have*, not as something one *does* by expending one's energies or one's time. It presents work as an asset one should be prepared to make sacrifices to 'possess'; an asset for whose 'creation' (for work is no longer seen as creating wealth, but wealth as creating jobs) employers, owners, investors and companies deserve the encouragement and recompense of the nation, together with subsidies, incentives and tax concessions from the Inland Revenue. Work is a commodity, employment a privilege. And a rarer and rarer privilege, for 'there is going to be a shortage of work' and, whatever your skills, there's a danger you'll have to 'go without' it before long.

This is an enormous fraud. There is not and never will be 'enough work' (enough paid, steady, full-time employment) for everyone any longer, but society (or, rather, capital), which no longer needs everyone's labour, and is coming to need it less and less, keeps on repeating that it is not society which needs work (far from it!), but you who need it, and that it is going to strive – and strive mightily – to find, obtain or invent work for you: *work it could easily do without, but which you need absolutely.*

A wonderful inversion, this. It is no longer those who work who 'make themselves useful' to others, but society which is going to make itself useful by 'enabling' you to work, by 'giving' you that 'precious commodity' of work, in order as much as possible to avoid your 'going without' it. And the society which does this is the same one which is astonished and indignant when those who have been granted the 'privilege' of working have the gall to debate, or even reject, the increasingly oppressive working conditions imposed on them at ever decreasing wage rates.

Never has the ideology of work-as-value been proclaimed, flaunted, reiterated so unashamedly and never has capital's – business's – domination of the conditions and price of labour been so undisputed. Never has the 'irreplaceable', 'indispensable' function of labour as the source of 'social ties', 'social cohesion', 'integration', 'socialization', 'personalization', 'personal identity' and meaning been invoked so obsessively as it has since the day it became unable any longer to fulfil *any* of these functions – nor any of the five structural functions Marie Yahoda identified for it in her famous study of the unemployed of Marienthal in the early 1930s. Having become insecure, flexible, intermittent, variable as regards hours and wages, employment no longer integrates one into a community, no longer structures the daily, weekly or annual round, or the stages of life, and is no longer the foundation on which everyone can base his/her life project.

The society in which everyone could hope to have a place and a future marked out for him/her – the 'work-based society', in which he/she could hope to have security and usefulness – is dead. Work now retains merely a phantom centrality: phantom in the sense of a phantom limb from which an amputee might continue to feel pain. We are a society of phantom work, spectrally surviving the extinction of that work by virtue of the obsessive, reactive invocations of those who continue to see work-based society as the only possible society and who can imagine no other future than the return of the past. Such people do everyone the worst service imaginable by persuading us that there is no possible future, sociality, life or self-fulfilment outside employment; by persuading us that the choice is between a job and oblivion; between inclusion through employment and exclusion; between 'identity-giving socialization through work' and collapse into the 'despair' of non-being. They persuade us it is right, normal, essential that *'each of us should urgently desire'* what in actual fact no longer exists and will never again lie within everyone's grasp: namely, 'paid work in a permanent job', as the 'means of access to both social and personal identity', as 'a unique opportunity to define oneself and give meaning to one's life'.[2]

These obsessive invocations contribute powerfully to keeping some already outdated norms alive. They play their part in justifying and perpetuating as 'normal' expectations which are wholly out of touch with real developments; in condemning to distress and downcast impotence those whose 'rightful' expectations will inevitably be disappointed. They give succour to the power strategy of capital which – in order to be able to create 'flexibility' and insecurity, to individualize and select, to increase productivity and profits, and to reduce pay and staffing levels – needs precisely what those who sing the praises of the centrality of employment and its irreplaceable social functions offer it: namely, that everyone should continue 'urgently' to desire what companies will grant only to a few, so that the competition of each against all on the labour market will lower expectations and intensify the eager self-submission of the rare 'privileged individuals' whom companies will allow to serve them.

It is by reinforcing 'public opinion' in its unrealistic expectations, in its adherence to outdated norms, in stereotyped interpretations wholly out of step with the realities they claim to decipher that credence and sustenance are given to manichaean visions, scapegoat theories and proto-fascist ideologies and practices.

Critics will object, citing the opinion polls, that 'public opinion' is not yet ready to hear a different story; that the aspiration towards a life in which work is no longer central 'is not finally established';

in short, that the 'job or nothing' ideology represents the mindset of the majority and any other argument can be of interest only to 'cranks' or drop-outs.

This is a strange line of argument, which is not only based on a false premiss (as we shall see below), but amounts to saying that if the majority were to persist in believing the Earth were flat, we ought to reinforce that belief by concealing the evidence to the contrary. This sort of reasoning plays into the hands of the powerful by its *repressive function*, that is to say, by its desire to ignore, censure and repress any attempt to go to the heart of the matter. For the point now is not to ask *whether* individuals are capable of living a life no longer centred on employment, or whether they are ready for a society arranged in that way, but *how* that other life and society can be anticipated and prefigured right now in large-scale experiments, exemplary practices and struggles, alternative modes of co-operation, production, living space, self-providing for collective needs; *how* the fear of falling into the black hole of non-society and individual meaninglessness can be allayed by shared practices which devise and exemplify new forms of solidarity; *how*, instead of passively succumbing to dramatic technological change, 'savings' in working time, intermittent work patterns and job insecurity, we can seize upon these developments collectively, take the initiative and control them, turn them around against capital's strategists as potential sources of freedom; and *how* everyone can be assured of a continuous income when work is becoming increasingly discontinuous.

GENERATION X OR THE UNHEARD REVOLUTION

The society now being established through the inability to see and desire what lies beyond the currently disintegrating work-based society is an absolute non-society. The problem lies on the borders between the cultural and the political. For the economy and society to change, the mentality has to change. Conversely, that change of mentality, that cultural change need to be backed up by, and expressed in, political practices and a political project if they are to acquire a general import and find a collective expression capable of making itself publicly heard. So long as it has not found its collective, public expression, the shift in mentality can be ignored by the powerful, and regarded by them as marginal, deviant and insignificant.

The problem lies at this level, and with it the most urgent task before us, since, contrary to what those in power tell us, the change of mentality has already taken place. What is cruelly lacking is a public translation of its meaning and its latent radicalism. That translation cannot be accomplished spontaneously by a collective intelligence. It requires 'technicians of practical knowledge' (as Sartre called the 'organic intellectuals' of an emerging movement) who are capable of deciphering the meaning of a cultural change and identifying its themes in such a way that subjects can recognize their common aspirations. To succeed in that work of interpretation, observers/interpreters must be capable of breaking with interpretative and cultural stereotypes and raising themselves to a level of consciousness that is *at least equal to that of the most conscious subjects* whose experience they are interpreting.

Public opinion polls are, consequently, of no value until a prior work of interpretation and thematization has brought out the questions (the themes) to be put to the public. This is the old problem of the hermeneutic circle: we understand only what we know, and know only what we are capable of understanding. If we perceive and interpret the new in terms of the interpretative patterns and cultural stereotypes of the old, we remain blind to the respects in which it is new. If we interpret the aspiration to autonomy in terms of the norms of social conformism, we shall see it merely as deviance, withdrawal and selfishness. *Only a subject understanding him/herself to be such can recognize, understand and translate the labour of emancipation of other subjects, their efforts to produce themselves.*

In a period in which familiar values are losing their force, and social and professional 'roles', given their insecurity, changeability and lack of consistency, can no longer confer stable 'identities' on individuals, only a hermeneutics of the subject can enable sociology to decipher the endless quest to which subjects are condemned if they are to define themselves and give meaning and coherence to their existences.[3] The protagonists (in the etymological sense) are those who, instead of forlornly calling on society to provide a 'social role' that can satisfy their backward-looking yearnings for identity, themselves take on the work of producing sociality, themselves invent their daily solidarities, achieve their own socialization through a continual quest for what they share or can pool. The new protagonists are those people who, instead of passively putting up with the insecurity and discontinuity of most jobs, try to use these as a spring-board for their self-affirmation and for a richer, freer, more solidary life. They are the 'obscure heroes of insecurity',[4] the 'pioneers of chosen working hours'[5] who, 'in their daily resistance to economic reason bring out questions and answers, intentions and projects, and develop in actuality a politics of everyday life based on the freedom of action and the possibility of creating an organization for oneself and others which promotes autonomy'.[6]

In the initial stages, open-ended interviews and case histories cast more light on the cultural changes which are taking place than opinion polls could do. Such interviews provide the themes on which polls can be based, together with an interpretative grid for under-standing the responses. It was the pioneering work carried out in the USA by Daniel Yankelovich[7] which made possible and inspired the international research project undertaken by Rainer Zoll.[8] It was the Canadian writer Douglas Coupland who, in an international best-seller that was part investigative journalism, part novel, part social document, revealed the existence of – and named – Genera-tion X, the generation of those who refuse to 'be dead at 30, buried at 70'.[9] Like the young people in Germany studied by Zoll, they will not settle into any of the occupations for which they are suited because none of these has 'sufficient substance', none is sufficiently worthwhile. They prefer to 'hang loose', drifting from one tempo-rary 'McJob' to another, always retaining as much time as possible to follow the favoured activities of their tribe.

An international survey of young graduates in North America, Great Britain and the Netherlands some years later complemented Coupland's account. That survey found that:

> For many of these people, the promise of pension plans and career advancement based on full-time corporate loyalty is unattractive. They are both anticipating and pre-empting the insecurity of work . . . They demand varied, project-based work that will build on their expertise and increase their employability elsewhere. Unwilling to commit themselves to full-time, long-term corporate goals, 'Genera-tion X' no longer define themselves through reference to their employment. They have a personal agenda that is more important than that of the organization they work for, and they may be moti-vated by a sense of ethical value or genuine social utility – a 'worth-while ethic' rather than a work ethic. They value their autonomy, rank

'greater control over their time' as the third most important priority behind money and the utilizing of their intellectual faculties, and they 'want a better balance between work and other life interests – hobbies, leisure activities and in the future time spent with the family.'

What these studies demonstrate is people's growing readiness to question the purpose and utility of work, and of work-based society, on the basis of skills, interests, values and desires which pertain to individuals' experience of themselves as existing outside of, and even in opposition to, the work they are expected to perform.[10]

Two surveys carried out in France on young graduates of the Grandes Écoles confirm in every particular the conclusions of the international survey analysed here by Cannon. The first of these, conducted late in 1990 on the initiative of *Le Monde*, shows that:

> brilliant as they are, the young graduates, essentially selected to espouse the cause of efficiency and motivation . . . , withhold their full and entire commitment. They give their bodies, but not their souls, holding back on their effort in a way only the highly gifted can, while still creating the illusion of commitment: . . . They are tempted by quick careers, would happily 'throw it all up' for more authentic pleasures, wishing always to retire very early, if not indeed to be able to live off their savings. All in all, their aim is 'not to let the system grind them down'.[11]

> They wish to leave the rat race, and regard their qualifications as tools for promoting the aspirations they have in their personal lives, not especially as allowing them to occupy a role in the economy . . . When asked their definition of professional success, what comes out way ahead of everything else is the possibility of working when it suits them, so as to be able to devote more time to personal activities.[12]

Three years later, a survey of students at the prestigious École Polytechnique and of young graduates from that institution, published in *La Rouge et verte* (the periodical of the Association of Alumni), confirmed this disaffection regarding careers and the general preference for multi-activity and part-time working. 'The relation to work is growing looser because life goes on elsewhere', and particularly in 'unpaid activities which are regarded as socially useful'. 'It is only seldom now that companies seem like big families. Young people feel no compunction about changing employer', given that 'companies themselves are increasingly issuing short-term or work-experience contracts instead of employing people properly.' This gives rise to a purely instrumental perception of the 'job' as a means of earning a living. 'The company is regarded as a mere provider of wages . . . [It] conceals its true nature which is simply to be a profit centre in which people are mere human resources.'[13]

Contrary to the prevailing view, then, the intellectualization of work and occupations does not *of itself* bring about a growing involvement and identification of the whole person with his/her job. In fact, the opposite occurs. According to the survey of the young Polytechnique students, 'Employment becomes abstract or anonymous. You no longer see the end-product and the workers no longer derive any pride from it.'[14] Identification with the job is becoming incompatible with identification with the company.[15] Total involvement in what you do is becoming incompatible with the 'full-time employment' model. Between life and employment, between the person and his/her productive function, the gap is widening.

The company's declared aim of mobilizing the whole person to its advantage actually produces the opposite result: it is felt as a totalitarian oppression to which people tend to respond by withdrawing, by investing less of themselves: it produces the desire to counterbalance employment with self-determined activities, to have control of one's time, one's life, to determine its ends and how those ends are achieved. The possibility of working discontinuously, of combining employment with many and varied activities, is a goal pursued by the new 'elites of knowledge workers', as it was by nineteenth-century craft workers, but they are not alone in pursuing it.

The disaffection with '*work*' is spreading in all countries and throughout the entire working population, however obsessive the concern with finding a source of income or the fear of losing one's *job* are becoming. In Germany, only 10 per cent of the working population regard their work as the most important thing in their lives. In the United States, the proportion is 18 per cent, as against 38 per cent in 1955.[16] Among Western Europeans aged between 16 and 34, 'work' or 'a career' trail far behind five other priorities in the list of 'things which are really important to you personally', the five priorities being (1) having friends (95 per cent); (2) having enough free time (80 per cent); (3) being in good physical shape (77 per cent); (4) and (5) spending time with one's family and having an active social life (74 per cent).[17] Only 9 per cent of those questioned (7 per cent of young people between 13 and 25) cited work as 'the main factor for success in life'.[18] The gulf between 'work' and 'life' seems greater than ever: 57 per cent of Britons, for example, 'refuse to let work interfere with their lives', as against only 37 per cent of those aged between 45 and 54.[19] And in a sample of upper-middle-class, full-time employees in the USA, Juliet Schor finds 73 per cent of people take the view they would have a better quality of life if they worked less, spent less and had more time for themselves. An America-wide survey found that 28 per cent of those questioned had indeed chosen to 'downshift' (i.e. voluntarily earn and spend less) in order to lead a 'more meaningful' life.[20]

POLITICS LAGS BEHIND THE SHIFT IN VALUES

To put it simply, a cultural change has actually taken place. *Consequently, the problem does not lie where we normally think it does.* It does not lie in the difficulty of gaining acceptance for a lifestyle in which employment has a much smaller place within *everyone*'s life. It does not lie in everyone's identification with his/her job. It does not lie in 'everyone's urgent desire' to occupy a full-time job on a permanent basis. It does not lie in social attitudes not having caught up with the potential for a more relaxed, more multi-active life. It lies, rather, in *the political world not having caught up with the change in attitudes.* It lies in the fact that full economic, social and political rights (the rights to a full income and welfare benefits, and rights of collective action, representation and organization) remain attached only to those jobs which are occupied full-time on a regular basis – jobs which are increasingly rare. It lies in the danger that if you lose your stable employment, you might also lose your whole income, and all opportunities for activity and contact with others. And, as a consequence, *employment is valued as such*, not mainly for the satisfactions which *work* brings, but for the rights and entitlements attaching to the 'employment' form and to that form alone.

Now, once it becomes a source of rights and, consequently, of citizenship, employment itself appears to be a right which, given the general principle of equal rights, must be accessible to all citizens. The social usefulness (or uselessness) of work itself is transcended by the normative legal status of its employment form. The 'right to work' (synonymous with the right to employment) is demanded above all as a *political right* – as a right to accede to social and economic citizenship. So long as this is the case, activities deviating from the norm of regular, full-time work will be regarded as *inferior*, as tending to *deprive* citizens of their full rights, to *deny* them the rights and advantages which 'normally' employed persons enjoy. However desirable discontinuous working – with shorter hours and to a timetable chosen by the worker – may *in itself* be for the great majority of people taken individually, it is feared and rejected by many because it 'doesn't have the same status' and is a handicap to one's career.[21]

It is for all these reasons that the problem and its solution are first and foremost political:[22] they lie in the definition of new rights, new freedoms, new collective guarantees, new public facilities and new social norms, in terms of which chosen working time and chosen activities will no longer be marginal to society, but part of a new blueprint for society: a 'society of chosen time' and 'multi-activity'. A society which shifts the production of the social bond towards relations of co-operation, regulated not by the market and money, but by reciprocity and mutuality. A society in which all individuals can measure themselves against others, gain their esteem and demonstrate their value not mainly by their occupation and earnings but by a range of activities deployed in the public space and publicly acknowledged in other than monetary ways.

This blueprint for society (which I shall attempt to outline in more detail below) is much more in keeping with the general lines of technical and cultural change than the vain attempts to shore up wage-based society by extending the wage relation to activities not yet regulated by money. It corresponds to a situation in which capitalism dooms to social uselessness the growing mass of people for whom it no longer has any work, and in which society reveals itself incapable of *producing individuals to serve it or of using the individuals it produces. There is no longer enough society for individuals to be able to define themselves by their way of serving it. Instead of serving it, the point now is to produce it.*

The revolution is complete. Individuals are suddenly stripped of all their masks, roles, positions, identities and functions. These were not something they could confer upon themselves; and the fact that it was society which had allotted them actually exempted individuals – indeed, prevented them – from appearing to themselves as subjects. They are naked and alone now, with no protection from themselves, with neither obligations nor helpful restraints, abandoned by a society which no longer marks out their futures. Here they stand, faced with the task of having to construct themselves and build a different society in place of the one which is abandoning them: faced with the task which all societies – including the ones which are already in their death throes – fear most, for it requires, first and foremost, rebels, revolutionaries, resistance fighters, dissidents: that task being to free oneself from social roles and to 'become a Subject by abandoning the Self . . . [by resisting] the logic of social domination in the name of a logic of freedom and free self-production'. The 'obsessive search for identity', on the contrary, is but 'the self-destruction of the individual incapable . . . of becoming a subject'.[23]

For that incapacity there is no social remedy. Quite the contrary: it is itself social, socially produced and endlessly reproduced by that 'dominant social' discourse which continues to offer individuals images of themselves and conceptions of their roles which they cannot match up to. 'Subjectivation is always the antithesis of socialization,' writes Touraine.[24] It is entirely as though the notion of 'social usefulness' and the idea of social integration were being trotted out the more obsessively precisely as those elements which make a society capable of integration and of defining how everyone serves it were breaking up and disappearing. The notion of social usefulness is in reality as outdated as the notion of society itself; it is as obsolete as the idea that 'functionality is the criterion of the good'.[25] Society no longer exists, if by 'society' we understand a coherent whole assigning positions, functions and modes of belonging to its members. Individuals are no longer the means determined by society for its functioning. On the contrary, in the formulation of Christian Lalive d'Épinay, it is society which is called upon to become a means for the free development of the individual, or, more precisely, *the space in which each contributes to creating for all, and all for each, the conditions for a free development of their individuality.* The complete fulfilment of each individual now becomes the goal which society must make possible, and which itself makes possible a society in which concern for the fulfilment of the person is socially recognized and legitimated. In that society, the range of socially valued activities will go far beyond 'useful work'. The production of society will no longer take place mainly in the economic sphere, nor the production of self in employment.

This is the meaning of the cultural change which finds thematic expression in the feminist or ecological movements and in the concern for the quality of life and the environment. Common to all these is a rejection of the work ethic, self-abnegation, sacrifice, saving, obligatory commitment and 'putting life off until later'. They oppose instrumental reason – that is to say, the use of things and people as means to ends which are themselves means to other ends, and so on – in the name of an ethic of the care of self, of others, of other living creatures, of everything which requires protection and care. In this same vein, in a three-part series of articles on the future of the left, Anthony Giddens has suggested that socialism should be defined by the primacy accorded to the non-instrumental activities which embody 'an attitude of care':

> Care implies an ethics of responsibility, for oneself, for others and for the fabric of the material world. Care is the opposite of egoism, but shouldn't be equated with altruism. For care of the self – a responsible attitude towards self and body – is at the origin of the ability to care about, and for, others.[26]

The changes prompted by the upheavals introduced by capitalism in its latest phase go right to the basics of what modern societies have been thus far. They force us to redefine the nature of the 'social bond'; to redefine the relation between the individual and the social; critically to rethink the nature and process of 'socialization'; to change the places where, and the means by which, society is 'produced'. They render problematic everything which was familiar, routine and normal – everything which was 'taken for granted'. There is no room here for institutional solutions or 'top-down' answers which would exempt the 'administered' population from a self-critical questioning of the status quo.

SOCIALIZATION OR EDUCATION?

The idea that the reproduction of society is to be achieved by the socialization of individuals remains so firmly anchored in habits of thought that it survives the break-up of society and the disappearance of the social 'roles' for which socialization was appropriate. Most current social thinkers still argue as though the capacity of individuals to become autonomous subjects producing themselves and social ties by their non-instrumental activities could only be the product of 'successful socialization'. For Jean-Louis Laville, for example, 'the emphasis on free time is based on an assumption of individuals fitted for autonomy and responsibility, *that is to say*, individuals who have achieved a successful socialization, whereas it is that socialization which poses a problem.'[27]

In this ostensibly innocent statement, we find the ideological postulate of that same sociologism we also meet in Habermas and Parsons, among others.[28] In that conception, the aptitude for autonomy and responsibility are seen as the result of a 'successfully achieved socialization' or, in other words, the subject-individual is seen as the set of *social* capacities, skills and behaviours which society teaches individuals in order for those individuals to produce society. The subject (interiority in Hannah Arendt's more Hegelian vocabulary) is here evacuated; the 'subject' is now merely the support of social 'roles', sensibilities and skills which respond to the anonymous 'expectations' inscribed in the functioning of social processes. In this sociologistic conception, socialization is not an emancipation giving rise to a subject capable of autonomy, self-determination and judgement. On the contrary, it masks the subjects' power to produce themselves by assigning them a personality which they cannot experience as their innermost self: 'Ego' is another; whereas 'I' is aware of the otherness of the Self and contests it.

The confusion between 'Ego' and 'I' comes in large measure from the way sociologism, colonizing and supplanting philosophical thinking, conflates *education* with *socialization*. Admittedly, in so far as it necessarily includes the learning of a language, codes and socio-cultural references, any education is *also* socialization. But it is not just that. And we can even say that it is incapable of educating *and* socializing if it aspires to be only that. Unlike conditioning, indoctrination and training, education aims essentially at bringing out in individuals the autonomous capacity to take charge of themselves, that is to say, the capacity to become the subject of their relation to themselves, the world and others. This cannot be *taught*; it has to be *stimulated*. It can arise only out of the affective attachment of children or adolescents to a reference person who makes them *feel* deserving of *unconditional* love, and *confident* of their capacity to learn, act, undertake projects and measure themselves against others – who gives them, in a word, 'self-esteem'. The subject emerges by virtue of the love with which another subject calls it to become a subject and it develops through the desire to be loved by that other subject.

This means that *the educative relation is not a social relation and is not socializable*. It is successfully achieved only if the child is an incomparably singular being for the person educating him/her, a being loved for him/herself and to be revealed to him/herself by that love as *entitled to his/her singularity*: that is to say, as a subject-individual. The maternal or paternal 'function' (or that of the adoptive parent, whether brother, aunt, grandfather, etc.) is not socializable, for we are dealing here not with a function, but with a loving relationship which society always regards with suspicion or downright hostility. That function threatens to make children rebels by educating (e-ducating) them to be in charge of their own existences as autonomous subjects, instead of inculcating in them society's right to take control of them (as school, army and party do).

Love is not a social sentiment, nor education a 'social function'. Educators or teachers know this, coming into conflict as they always do sooner or later with society, institutions or administrations, and with *over-socialized* parents, to the precise degree to which they feel it is their vocation not to give the child to society, by inculcating conformity to norms, but to give the child *to him/herself* by imparting self-esteem.

Socialization does, indeed, 'pose a problem', as Laville says, but for reasons opposite to those he suggests. It is the excess of socialization, not the lack of it, which puts a block on individual autonomy. More precisely, what creates that block is the priority which worried parents accord to socialization through schooling over genuine education; to success at school over full sensory and emotional development; to the acquisition of social 'skills' over the development of the imaginative and creative faculties, the capacity to take control of one's life and achieve self-esteem outside the prescribed paths. Socialization will continue to produce frustrated, ill-adapted, mutilated, disorientated individuals so long as it persists in emphasizing 'social integration through employment', to the exclusion of all else, and investing all its efforts in integrating people into a 'society of workers', in which all activities are considered as 'ways of earning one's living'.[29]

What we have here once again is the opposition between the thinking of political philosophy (always axiomatic in tendency) on the good society and the good life, on the one hand, and functionalist thinking on the other. What counts for the former is 'the labour through which an individual transforms him or herself into an actor

... capable of transforming a situation rather than reproducing it through his mode of behaviour'.[30] What counts for the latter is the formation of 'social individuals' possessing the social skills and behaviour which make them fitted to fulfil the functions or roles which the process of social labour defines for them. The former are interested in social movements inasmuch as it is their aim to seize the spaces which become vacant in the wake of the decomposition of society, abolish that society and replace it by another. The latter are interested in the institutional means for perpetuating the work-based society by revamping it, reforming it and adapting individuals to new types of jobs.

The former stress that 'people have to be prepared, from school-days onwards, to live through periods of unemployment in which many voluntary activities will be able to flourish';[31] whilst, among the latter, the dominant concern is to professionalize, to 'capitalize' interpersonal 'skills', to transform the 'most specifically human qualities' into employment;[32] 'to drag the most fundamental human relationships into the ambit of professional time'.[33] We are back here, at another level, with the debate initiated by Paolo Virno on 'putting to work those things which are most common, i.e. intellect and speech', a process he sees as 'the acme of subjugation'. 'No one is quite so poor as the person who sees his relations to others or his language abilities reduced to the status of paid work'; or, rather, nothing is more impoverishing for a culture than to see the most spontaneous affective bonds between people – sympathy, empathy, compassion, attention, communication, etc. – 'objectified in training and qualifications'[34] and used to satisfy an employer or gain a client, used for 'knowing how to sell oneself' to the former, and how to sell things to the latter.[35]

One might, of course, retort that personalizing the relationship between service provider and customer 'adds a non-commercial dimension to work' and a personal element to commercial transactions. But for it to be so, the salesperson's kindliness, attentiveness and patience would have to be spontaneous and disinterested. In that case, we are speaking of attitudes that can neither be taught nor objectively enshrined in qualifications. If pleasant and attentive attitudes are taught and studied, and such attributes are embodied in examination certificates as the 'social skills' required to make a sale or clinch a deal, they cease to be spontaneous and fall under the same suspicion of hypocrisy and self-interest as that 'commercial smile' and standardized, superficial bonhomie for which we routinely criticize Americans. The professionalization of 'inter-personal skills' as a means of expanding employment poisons our day-to-day culture and eats away at the arts of living. If massive savings in working time are to lead to a civilization in which life flourishes as an end in itself and in which the production of self and the production of sociality prevail over the sale of self, it is vernacular, spontaneous skills that need to be developed, not their professionalization.

I know that all this cannot be changed overnight. I also know that we have to act quickly, for 'de-socialization' is advancing even more rapidly than mass unemployment and poverty. I know too that, for twenty-five years, the pressing need for action has served as an alibi for not addressing the roots of the matter. *It is time now to come at these questions from the opposite direction: instead of limiting our goals to stop-gap measures achievable with readily available means, let us start by defining the ultimately attainable goal and determine what changes are required to achieve it.* It is to this that I now turn.

4
Moving Beyond Wage-Based Society

MULTI-ACTIVITY AS A KEY SOCIAL ISSUE

The imperative need for a sufficient, regular income is one thing. The need to act, to strive, to test oneself against others and be appreciated by them is quite another. Capitalism systematically links the two, conflates them, and upon that conflation establishes capital's power and its ideological hold on people's minds. It admits no activity which is not 'work', done to order and paid for by those ordering it. It admits no regular income that is not earned from 'work'. *The imperative need for a regular income is used to persuade people of their 'imperative need to work'.* The need to act, to strive, to be appreciated is used to persuade people that they need to be paid for whatever they do.

Because social production (both of the necessary and of the superfluous) demands less and less work and distributes less and less in wages, it is becoming increasingly difficult to obtain a sufficient, regular income from paid work. In 'capital-speak', this difficulty is attributed to the 'shortage of work'. This masks the real situation. The actual problem is not a shortage of work, but a failure to distribute the wealth which is now produced by capital employing fewer and fewer workers.

The remedy for this situation is clearly not to 'create work', but to distribute optimally all the socially necessary work and all the socially produced wealth. The effect of this will be that what capitalism has artificially conflated can once again be put asunder: the right to a sufficient, regular income will no longer have to depend on the permanent occupation of a steady job. The need to act, strive and be appreciated by others will no longer have to take the form of paid work done to order. Such work will take up less and less time in the life of society and in everyone's lives. People will be able to divide their lives between a wide range of activities, which will have neither payment nor profitability as their necessary condition or goal. Social relations, co-operative bonds and the meaning of each life will be mainly produced by these activities which do not valorize capital. *Working time will cease to be the dominant social time.*

These are, put very broadly, the outlines of the society and the civilization which are struggling to be born beyond the wage-based society. They correspond to the cultural changes which are currently taking place. They correspond to the aspiration for a multi-active life within which each person can give work its limited place, instead of relegating 'life' to the limited time allowed for it by the constraints of 'work'. However, this new scenario presupposes a political break equal to the ideological break the current cultural changes confusedly reflect. It presupposes that the need to act and be socially recognized succeed in freeing itself from paid 'work' done to order; that work free itself from the domination of capital; that persons free themselves from the domination of work to fulfil themselves in the wide range of their varied activities. In short, it presupposes that an end be put to the conflation on which capital bases its ideological grip and its power.

The heart of the problem and the stakes in the central conflict can be summed up in the following alternative: either work can be integrated into a multi-active life as one of its components, or multi-activity can be integrated into 'work' as one of its forms. Either working time can be integrated into the differentiated temporality of a multi-dimensional life, in keeping with current dominant cultural aspirations, or the rhythms of life can be subjected to capital's need for profitability and companies' need for 'flexibility'. In a word, we can either subordinate the apparatus and the social process of production to the power of living activities, or we can enslave those activities the more completely to that apparatus and that process. Behind the question of power over time, it is power *tout court* that is at issue: the distribution of power throughout society, and the direction in which society is to move. Rights over time, over periods of time for diversified activity, are the stakes in a cultural conflict which inevitably spills over into a political conflict.

That conflict is not a new one. What is new is that it is tending to become both inevitable and central. The multi-activity to which a majority of working people aspire 'culturally' does not merely correspond to their individual and private desires and aspirations. It is not simply the form taken by individuals' aspirations towards autonomy. It is the subjectivization of a capacity for autonomy which the 'economy of the immaterial' – and companies themselves – demand of personnel. It is that capacity for autonomy which, in the aspiration towards multi-activity, working people are tending to claim for themselves, beyond the limits their companies set for it and beyond the need those companies have of it. The power struggle then becomes inevitable and relates to the status of that autonomy and its scope – autonomy's *rights over itself*: the rights of persons to and over themselves. It relates, in a word, to *the autonomy of autonomy*, considered and valued not, in this case, as a necessary means, subjugated to the imperatives of competition and profit, but as the cardinal value on which all others rest and against which they are measured. The issue, in a nutshell, is *the development of people's autonomy irrespective of companies' need for it*. What is at stake is the possibility of withdrawing from the power of capital, of the market, of the economic sphere, the fields of activity which are opening up in the time freed from work.

We find an exemplary illustration of this issue in two schemes for 'pluri-activity' or 'multi-activity' which have been submitted for public debate in France. The first of these takes the typical employers' line and sees people's – carefully circumscribed – autonomy as a means of increasing the flexibility and productivity of their work. The second assumes an explicitly political dimension by conceiving 'multi-activity' as a social issue: in this vision, it is to shift the centre of gravity of everyone's lives so that, from now on, business and work for economic ends have only a subordinate place.

1. The first of these schemes was developed in a report (the 'Boissonnat Report') of the Commissariat général du Plan on 'Work in Twenty Years' Time'. Picking up on the idea of 'pluri-activity', which had been discussed previously in management circles, this report envisaged companies being able to offer their staff so-called

'activity contracts'. The main function of these contracts would be to preserve the bond between workers and 'their' companies when their companies did not need their work for a limited period. The main aim of the 'activity contract' is to increase the 'flexibility' of the workforce and make employment more discontinuous without it becoming either insecure or temporary.

This is an aim which could be achieved in one of two ways. The first of these is to have several companies pool their permanent staff. (This is what is meant by 'pluri-activity' as originally discussed by the employers.) When one or other of the companies concerned cannot keep all its employees busy full-time, it can lend some of these to associated companies with a temporary labour shortage. In short, the plan is for a number of companies to get together to manage their staff jointly so as to ensure they are utilized most rationally, and to manage fluctuations in demand without systematic recourse to the use of contract or temporary labour.

The Boissonnat Report extends this notion of 'pluri-activity' to new areas. When a group of companies has no need of all its employees, it would be able to lend its temporary surplus of labour to 'other public or private bodies: local communities, schools, various associations' or put them on 'social utility leave (e.g. family leave)' or on training leave.[1]

Do not imagine, however, that the staff who were sent on leave in this way would be able to choose their non-professional activities freely, broaden their interests and skills, enrich their lives and those of their communities. The Report's authors make clear that 'the various forms of work, including training and freelance or voluntary activity' must be consonant with the 'collective or particular interests of the contracting companies'.[2] Although they are on 'social utility' leave, then, the workers must remain in the service of their companies even in their chosen voluntary work or cultural activity. They will remain in thrall to the logic, and the control, of their employers, confined during the breaks in their professional lives within the narrow horizon of productivism. 'The autonomy of the person' is itself instrumentalized here for its 'productive usefulness'.[3] In the end, the 'activity contract' extends the domination of productivist logic and subordination to company interests to those activities outside work which might otherwise be fitted in between periods of employment.

2. The Centre des jeunes dirigeants (CJD) proposes a fundamentally different approach. To the employers' notion of 'pluri-activity', it opposes a formula which allows 'each individual to regain control of their time'. This reappropriation, they argue, will represent the 'true wealth of the coming decades' and will be able to 'put an end to subjection to the economic sphere . . . If we wish to redistribute to all citizens this capacity to dispose of their time-capital, they have to be liberated from the subjection to rigid time schedules – from the need to spend their lives earning a living'.[4]

The CJD's formula, which is very close to the one I have myself proposed, allows for both an overall and an individualized reduction of working time (the former over a year or several years, the latter over a week or month, with each worker being able to choose and adjust his/her working hours) within a framework of 'permanent negotiation'. The company maintains 'security of income and status for employees' or, in other words, assures them of the right to a continuous income for discontinuous working, which may be organized on a basis they themselves select. The right to 'choose one's working hours' will necessarily lead to a new approach to work, 'which will set each of us on the way to other modes of participation in collective life, in society'.[5] 'The company will have to lose the excessive importance waged work has given it in people's lives . . . A complete overhaul of the organization of work, both within companies and in society generally' will be needed to provide the impetus for a whole set of changes.[6] The work-based society will have to give way to a society based on 'multi-activity'. 'The response to unemployment, and the exclusion and need for resocialization it produces, necessarily involve a rise in multi-activity and a diversification of social allegiances.' Hence the need to diversify sources of income: 'Business owes it to society right now to break the hold of employment by allowing people to enter gradually, at their own pace, into the logic of multi-activity . . . Conversely, it is up to society . . . to create the appropriate legal and political framework'.[7]

The starting point in this instance is an expressly political consideration. 'Multi-activity' and reducing the 'excessive importance' work and the company have assumed are presented as *a common aspiration which is to find collective expression and political realization through social change*. That change is necessary for the survival (or reconstitution) of a society in which both persons and companies can flourish by making the best of the innovative character of the productive forces. That society must be so constituted that, far from bringing about social disintegration, flexible, discontinuous and evolutional forms of working give rise to new forms of sociality and cohesion.

Whatever its limitations in other respects, the CJD distances itself here from the dominant thinking by clearly bringing out that *the fundamentally different society 'the twenty-first-century company' needs will come about only if it imposes itself independently of the companies' need for such a society.* That 'multi-activity and agreed time'-based society must impose itself through its intrinsic desirability. It must impose itself *by virtue of the aspirations by which the autonomous and 'rich individualities', which the companies need, transcend their productive function and become irreducible to that function.*

We have, in short, to rethink society on the lines of the aspirations which arise from the increased autonomy of persons, instead of conceiving it in terms of capital's need to shackle and control that autonomy. There is one important consequence of this approach to the political task: the social conditions through which, as we have seen, the post-Fordist enterprise 'subjects' the workers whom it no longer has power to command will have to disappear and, with them, the hold they gave capital over labour. The CJD's thinking on this aspect echoes the 'general intellect' theory:

> The source of value today lies in intelligence and imagination. Value is embodied in immaterial things. Human knowledge counts for more than machine time. Man, as bearer of his own knowledge capital, is bearer of part of the company's capital.
>
> This transformation of value will have important consequences in the future. The ownership of capital will become more and more distinct from that of the company. The company will have to be given a personality distinct from that of the formal joint-stock company. Insofar as [everyone] will possess an increasing share of the knowledge, and hence of the value of the company, it will be necessary to negotiate the daily organization and operation jointly – together with the most strategic decisions. Who will be able in the future to see themselves as owners of the company?[8]

Let us make no mistake about this: wage-labour has to disappear and, with it, capitalism.

When its implications and consequences are fully thought through, the multi-activity-based society is not a modified version of the 'work-based society'. It marks a breakthrough to a quite different form. If such a society is to be established and multi-activity to develop, more will be needed than society creating 'the legal and political framework for it'; or 'companies [having] broken the hold of employment'. For multi-activity to develop, *society will have to organize itself to achieve it through a range of specific policies*. Social time and space will have to be organized to indicate the general expectation that everybody will engage in a range of different activities and modes of membership of the society. To indicate that the norm is for everyone to belong – or at least to be able to belong – to a self-providing co-operative, a service exchange network, a scientific research and experiment group, an orchestra or a choir, a drama, dance or painting workshop, a sports club, a yoga or judo group, etc.; and that the aim within the sports or arts 'societies' is not to select, eliminate or rank individuals, but to *encourage each member to refresh and surpass him/herself ever anew in competitive co-operation with the others, this pursuit of excellence by each being a goal common to all.* This is how the 'culture-based' society (for which the Western prototype was Athenian society) is distinguished from the work-based society.

EXIT ROUTES

I shall now try to outline that 'set of specific policies' which, breaking with the work-based society, could open this up into a society based on multi-activity and culture. This is an experimental, exploratory attempt, pursuing goals similar to those embodied in the 'revolutionary reforms' which some of us proposed in the early 1960s:

1   First of all, we have to free up people's minds and imaginations, to cast off those unquestioned assumptions which the dominant social discourse latches on to. We have to think through those exemplary experiences which explore other forms of productive co-operation, exchange, solidarity and living.

2   We have to adopt the point of view of the radically different society and economy, which are visible on the horizon of the current changes and represent the ultimate potential destiny of the society that is currently disintegrating. This will force us, on

the one hand, to get a better grasp of the meaning of those changes and the outlines of what is struggling to be born. It will compel us, on the other, to understand that we are living not through a 'crisis' which could be resolved by the restoration of previous conditions, but though a transformation in which capitalism is itself destroying the foundations of its existence and producing the conditions for its own transcendence. But we still have to know how to seize upon those conditions and think through the transition by starting out from its ultimate conceivable term. It is only in the light of that ultimate state that we can judge what we do – or fail to do.

3   Lastly, we have to 'widen as far as possible the gap between society and capitalism',[9] that is to say, to increase as far as possible the spaces and resources which enable alternative socialities to be produced, which allow modes of life, co-operation and activities to emerge that lie outside the power apparatuses of capital and the state. In other words, we have to maximize the number of paths 'out of capitalism', this expression being understood in the sense of a biblical Exodus which invents its own 'promised lands' as it goes along.

The institutional actors who can decide to implement these policies will not be the actors in the alternative society which is struggling to come into existence. All we can ask of politics is to create the spaces in which the alternative social practices can develop. It is from this perspective that a politics which allows for, and encourages, multi-activity must be assessed, multi-activity being both the engine of the exodus and its final goal, in so far as this diminishes the importance of the wage relation, and opposes 'work' by substituting different modes of co-operation for it. As we shall see below in relation to a policy aim of 'changing the city', the change of mentalities is hastened by that of the social environment which in its turn gains momentum from the change of mentalities. System theorists call these effects, which generate the cause that generates them, a 'feedback loop'.

Fausto Bertinotti provided quite a good formulation of all this, without exaggerating the role a political party can play in:

the revolutionary alternative which . . . represents potentially a long process of social transformation, combining a break with the past, new organizations of subjectivity, the construction of concrete experiences and 'exemplary' institutional levels, and the ability to develop new theories . . . Proposals for a different economic and social policy . . . must *bring into play* both the elements of a possible 'What is to be Done?' and the outline of a 'different society', a 'different development', and 'other types of interpersonal relations', bringing together in a common perspective aspirations and levels of experience which will otherwise be expressed only in separate fragments incapable of communicating with each other.[10]

These aspirations and experiences involve new social relations lying beyond the logic of the market, money and the sexual division of labour; new areas of time outside the sphere of wage-labour; new production techniques and new relations to the environment respecting natural balances and other life forms, etc. And, at the heart of all this, the individual and collective reappropriation of time and its organization.

It is important to show that *the possibility of transcending capitalist society is inherent in the evolution of capitalist society itself.* You have to demonstrate that something is possible for it to become so. It is in this spirit that I shall now outline that 'set of policies' I alluded to above. Each of these is desirable in itself, but assumes its true meaning only when combined with, and supported by, the others. Each already exists in embryonic form. None has such a large initial cost that it cannot be applied with sufficient vigour to set its own dynamic running. But each taken in isolation can be exploited by the dominant powers in a way which will discredit it. I shall outline a set of policies aimed at:

1   guaranteeing a sufficient income for all;
2   combining the redistribution of work with the individual and collective control over time;
3   encouraging new socialities to blossom, and new modes of co-operation and exchange, through which social bonds and social cohesion will be created beyond the wage-relation.

Guaranteed income

Security of income is the first precondition for a society based on multi-activity. Unconditionally guaranteeing everyone an income for life will, however, have a fundamentally different meaning and function depending on whether that income is (1) insufficient or (2) sufficient for protecting him/her from poverty.

(1)   The guarantee of a basic income at less than subsistence level, which its advocates hope to see substituted for most forms of income redistribution (family allowance, housing, unemployment and sickness benefits, basic state pension, etc.), functions to force the unemployed to accept dirty, low-status jobs on the cheap. This is the position of the 'Friedmannite' neo-liberals of the Chicago School, and also of German liberals like Mitschke and of the British conservatives. In their view, unemployment is explained by the fact that many potential jobs with low skill levels and low productivity are unprofitable at normal rates of pay. These jobs have, consequently, to be subsidized by allowing the worker to combine an insufficient basic social income with an equally insufficient income from work. In this way, a kind of 'secondary labour market' is created, protected from competition from low-wage countries but 'protected' also from the provisions of labour legislation, which is destined to disappear. The lower the basic income, the greater will be the 'encouragement' to take any work at all, and the more new 'slavers' will be able to specialize in employing a cheap workforce in fly-by-night operations providing service work on a contract and subcontract basis.

American workfare, which received President Clinton's imprimatur in late July 1996, links the right to a very small welfare allowance with the obligation to perform unpaid – or very low-paid – work of 'social utility' for a municipal authority or approved association. Workfare has many advocates in France and Britain – and in Germany, where municipal authorities have begun to threaten the long-term unemployed with the withdrawal of their benefits if they do not perform work of 'public utility' (cleaning, earth-moving, clearance work, etc.), for which they are paid an hourly rate of 2 DM, which is intended to cover their travel and clothing expenses.

All forms of workfare stigmatize the unemployed as incompetents and scroungers, whom society is entitled to force to work – for their own good. In this way, it reassures itself as to the cause of unemployment: that cause is the unemployed themselves. They do not have, it is said, the social skills and requisite will-power to get a job, and they will consequently be put to the most menial tasks. In reality, the high rate of unemployment among the unskilled is due not to their lack of professional skills, but to the fact that (both in France and in Germany) one-third of skilled or highly skilled people are in unskilled occupations (for want of being able to find anything better) and have thus elbowed out those who ought normally to be able to fill those jobs. Instead of subsidizing unskilled jobs by way of a basic income, it is the redistribution of skilled jobs that ought to be subsidized by considerably lowering the hours of work in those occupations.

The ultra-conservative conception of workfare does, however, co-exist with a post-Fordist conception, defended by Yoland Bresson among others. Bresson advocates a universal, unconditional 'subsistence income' [*revenu d'existence*] of 1,800 French francs (c.£180) per month which would perform the function both of a total or partial unemployment benefit and of an incentive to accept casual part-time jobs with variable wages and hours. 'The future is one of discontinuous employment, and we have to give everyone the means to fit themselves into the new system . . . In this context, the sub-sistence income is a means, not an end in itself.'[11]

According to this conception, the 'subsistence income' is to *enable* employment to become intermittent, and may even *encourage* such intermittent employment. But who is to benefit from it? That is the question. A very low 'subsistence income' is in fact a subsidy for employers. It allows them to find labour while paying less than subsistence-level wages. But while it is enabling for the employers, it is an imposition upon the workers. Since they are not guaranteed a sufficient basic income, they have to look continually for some kind of casual work or temporary job and are, therefore, incapable of living their lives on a multi-activity basis. In this case, the 'subsis-tence income' gives a sizeable boost to deregulating the wage rela-tion, to making employment more insecure and 'flexible', and to replacing it with a commercial contract. We see here the traps inher-ent in demanding continuous income for discontinuous work. Unless, of course, *the breaks in work, its discontinuity, reflect not capital's discretionary power over labour, but the individual and collec-tive right of those performing work to control how they manage their own time.* We shall return to this below.

(2)   Granting each citizen a *sufficient* social income follows an oppo-site logic: the aim is not to force the recipients to accept any kind

of work on any terms whatsoever, but to free them from the constraints of the labour market. The basic social income must enable them to refuse work and reject 'inhuman' working conditions. And it must be part of *a social environment which enables all citizens to decide on an ongoing basis between the use-value of their time and its exchange-value*: that is to say between the 'utilities' they can acquire by selling their working time and those they can 'self-provide' by using that time themselves.

Such a universal grant of a sufficient income (I shall return to this at greater length below) must not be understood as a form of assistance, nor even of social protection, leaving individuals dependent upon the welfare state. It must be understood, rather, as a prime example of what Anthony Giddens calls a 'generative policy'.[12] That is to say, it must give individuals and groups increased resources for taking charge of their own lives, further power over their way of life and living conditions. The aim is not to enable people not to work at all, but rather to give genuine effect to the right to work: not the right to that work you are 'employed' to do, but to the concrete work you do without having to be paid for it, without its profitability or exchange-value coming into the equation.

The granting of a sufficient basic income to all citizens must, therefore, be inseparable from developing and making accessible the resources which enable and encourage self-activity to take place, the resources with which individuals and groups can satisfy by their own unshackled efforts part of the needs and desires they have themselves defined. This is why discussions of the precise amount of a sufficient income have no great meaning in themselves: they distract from the essence of the question which the current social changes really raise by situating those changes within the framework of wage-based society and seeking to finance the universal grant by fiscal redistribution. Now, the prospect which lies before us and which should be the backdrop to our thinking is a future with less employment and less selling of labour and services, but with a growth in collective facilities and services, in non-monetary exchange and self-providing. According to Frithjof Bergmann, high-tech self-providing could easily cover 70 per cent of needs and desires on two days' work a week.

The schemes which are currently being debated could move us closer to that ultimate goal or further from it; they could open up this potential future or close it off; they could show up the need for a break with the present system or by-pass that need. It is on this basis that they have to be judged.

It was, indeed, in this spirit that the universal grant of a sufficient social income was advocated by libertarian communists and socialists, whose aim was not to redistribute or 'share' employment, but to abolish wage-labour and the compulsion to work, to sweep away capitalist business and the state. These included Bellamy and Popper-Lynkeus at the dawn of the twentieth century, the French 'distributists' who followed Jacques Duboin's theories; the Proudhonite 'Ordre Nouveau' intellectual movement of Robert Aron, Arnaud Dandieu and Alexandre Marc in the 1930s; Paul Goodman in the USA in the 1950s; and at least some of the German 'Greens' who, in the 1980s, rediscovered this tradition and adapted some of its ideas to present conditions.

For many years I rejected the idea of a social income which would allow people to 'live without working'. This I did for reasons quite contrary to the disciples of Rawls, who see 'work' as 'a good' which must, in the name of justice, be distributed equitably. But 'work' is not 'a good'. It is a necessary activity, carried out in the modern period according to norms defined by society, at the demand of society, imparting a sense that one is capable of doing what society needs. It gives recognition, socializes and confers rights because it is itself required as an obligation. In this way, 'work' draws people out of their private solitude; it is an aspect of citizenship. And it represents, more fundamentally (as work one does) – beyond its particular social determination – a mastery of self and of the surrounding world which is necessary for the development of human capacities.

As the need for work diminishes, fairness requires that it should also diminish in everyone's life and that the burden of work should be equitably distributed. This is why, in previous works, I wanted the guarantee of a full income for all to be linked to all citizens performing the quantity of work required for the production of the wealth to which their income entitled them. This could take the form, for example, of 20,000 hours which individuals could spread over their working lives in as many 'tranches' as they wished, on condition that the gap between two working periods did not exceed a certain interval.

This formula, which I advocated from 1983 onwards, was consistent with the prospect of wage-labour and the 'law of value' disappearing: the guaranteed social income was no longer a wage.[13] It was consistent with taking back, and gaining control of, time. But it was not consistent with the perspectives opened up, and the changes brought about, by post-Fordism. I am therefore abandoning it for the following four reasons.

In defence of unconditionality

(1)   When intelligence and imagination ('general intellect') become the main productive force, working time ceases to be the measure of labour; indeed, it ceases to be measurable. The use-value produced may bear no relation to the time taken to produce it. It may vary greatly from person to person, or depending on the material or immaterial nature of the work. Lastly, stable employment paid according to the number of working hours per week is in rapid decline. It is becoming increasingly difficult to define an irreducible *quantity* of work to be performed by each person over a determinate period. It is impossible to measure the working hours of the self-employed or of craftworkers or the providers of intangible services. Only the granting of a basic social income can encourage these people – in most cases it is the only thing that can allow them – to reduce their professional activity in order to lead a multi-active life. Only the payment of a basic income will absolve them of the need to fight, in a crowded labour market, for the few crumbs from the ever smaller sums employers distribute to pay for labour. The *universal, unconditional* grant of a basic income is, therefore (in a context which I shall specify in detail below), the best instrument for redistributing both paid work and unpaid activities as widely as possible.

(2)   The *unconditional* right to a sufficient basic income will doubtless bring some immediate objections. How can we avoid a growing mass of scroungers living off the work of others? Won't those others refuse to carry the burden and demand the prohibition of such idling? Won't they call for work to be made compulsory in the form of workfare or obligatory community service?

Many advocates of a universal grant, both liberal and socialist, make these objections. But they then run up against the following difficulty: what is to be the content of the compulsory work to be demanded in return for the basic living allowance? How is that work to be defined, measured and distributed when the importance of work in the economy is declining? And how are they to avoid compulsory work competing with, and even destroying, an increasing proportion of normally paid public activities and jobs?

Claus Offe and Jeremy Rifkin respond, with others, by situating this compulsory work in the third sector of activities which meet needs that cannot be paid for, or profitably carried on, within the market economy. It is to be 'voluntary care work or educational activities, community work with approved associations'. In this way, the universal allowance would serve to create 'a post-industrial domestic sector'.[14] It would become the payment for voluntary work performed for recognized non-profit-making bodies. It would make 'voluntary' work compulsory.

Diane Elson makes a similar proposal: 'Alongside the right to a grant should be the duty, on the part of able-bodied adults, of undertaking some unpaid household work of caring and providing for those who are unable to take care of themselves. Persons already undertaking care of a young or old or sick or handicapped person would be exempt.'[15]

So, in the one case (Offe), the concern to have a *quid pro quo* in terms of work which does not compete with normal employment produces the nonsensical prospect of compulsory voluntary work. The perverse effects of this provision are clear for all to see: real volunteers would have alongside them 'pressed' volunteers, and there is every likelihood these latter would be treated as second-class workers and given the least rewarding work, since they would be doing the same things as the real volunteers were doing from conviction and for free, but would appear to be doing it (or would be suspected of doing it) simply in order to draw their allowance. Compulsory voluntary work then becomes a trap: it devalues the work of the volunteers who are pressed into doing it.

In the other case (Elson), the obligation on the recipients of a basic income to perform domestic work (intentionally) blurs the distinction between productive and reproductive labour. The latter is equated with the former and regarded as interchangeable with it. In this way, the private character of domestic activities is denied. Parents' obligations to their children, adults' obligations to their elderly parents would all be set up as social obligations and placed under public control. Spontaneous behaviour between persons – where spontaneity is, in fact, crucial to the emotional value – would be administratively monitored and standardized.[16]

In each case, the grant of a basic income is conceived as a payment for family activities which are thus irresistibly drawn into the field of those activities whereby one is called on to 'earn one's living'. Entitlement to the basic income requires either having children of one's own, or looking after other people's children and households, or working in the 'voluntary' sector. Activities whose normal meaning lies in an absence of self-interest become a means for acquiring an income. There is then no reason why the list of activities 'which may be regarded as work' should not extend to the artistic, cultural, religious or sporting fields.[17] If these kinds of activity themselves became a means to qualify for the basic income, they would in their turn be drawn within the ambit of instrumental reason and administrative standardization.

It is important that we grasp precisely what is at issue here. If we want the universal grant of a basic income to be linked to the performance of equivalent work as its justification, two conditions have to be met. First, that work has to be work within the public sphere which is of benefit to everyone, and, second, that work *must be able to have payment* (in this case, of the basic income) *as its aim, without the fact of payment corrupting its meaning*. If it is not possible to meet this latter condition, and if the universal grant is intended to promote voluntary, artistic, cultural, family and mutual-aid activities, then the universal grant has to be guaranteed to everyone unconditionally. For only if it is unconditional will it be possible to protect the unconditional nature of those activities which are only fully meaningful when done for their own sake. After arguing against it for many years, I have therefore come round to the position of those who advocate a *sufficient* (not a minimal) basic income which is 'strictly unconditional', as Alain Caillé and Ahmet Insel put it.[18] I see this as the only way to preserve the voluntary sector and to protect from socialization and economicization – while at the same time making them accessible to all – those activities 'which derive their value from being done for their own sake'.

(3)   The universal grant of a basic income is the most appropriate arrangement for a situation in which the 'general state of science' is coming to be the main force of production[19] and in which direct working time is becoming negligible by comparison with the time required for the production, reproduction and extended reproduction of the capacities and skills of the workforce in the so-called

'immaterial economy'. It would be interesting to calculate the number of weeks or years spent on basic and continuing training, in the training of trainers, etc. for each hour, week or year of direct work performed in the economy. And training itself is a small matter by comparison with all that it takes to provide for the development of the capacities of imagination, interpretation, analysis, synthesis and communication integral to the post-Fordist workforce. In the 'immaterial' economy, 'the worker is both the labour power and the one who directs that labour power'. It can no longer be detached from his/her person:

> Worker, work and labour power tend to merge in self-producing persons. And that production takes place not just in the workplace, but in schools, cafés, stadiums, neighbourhoods and discussion groups, on trips, at theatres and concerts, through newspapers and books etc. In short, it takes place wherever individuals come together and produce the world of social relations.[20]

In progressive firms, continuing training is already part of work (and working hours) and is paid for as such. But this extension of the employment contract to include training is not without its disadvantages, since it subordinates the right to training, and the nature of that training, to company interests. It develops a merely functional, limited autonomy in individuals, of a kind which can be controlled and subjected. By contrast, it is one of the functions of an unconditional basic income to make the right to develop one's capacities an unconditional right to an autonomy which transcends its productive function; an autonomy experienced and valued for its own sake on a variety of planes: moral (autonomy of value-judgement), political (autonomy of decision-making regarding the common good), cultural (invention of life-styles, consumption models and arts of living) and existential (the capacity to take care of oneself, rather than leave the experts and authorities to decide what is good for us).

Beyond the 'labour theory of value'

(4)   There is a further argument in favour of an unconditional social income. It is the arrangement best suited to the economy that is beginning to emerge on the other side of the impasse into which

current trends are leading. An increasing volume of wealth is produced with a decreasing volume of capital and labour. As a result, production distributes a decreasing amount of pay and wages to a decreasing number of workers. The purchasing power of a growing proportion of the population is falling. Unemployment, poverty and absolute destitution are spreading. The rapidly growing productivity of labour and capital produces a surplus of labour power and capital. And the latter now attempts to expand either without passing through the mediation of productive work at all (simply by transactions on the financial or currency markets) or by investing in low-wage countries. The contraction in the volume of wages – *and also the tax breaks which states accord capital to prevent its flight* – lead to a situation in which those activities and investments which do not bring short-term returns (research, education, public services and amenities, environmental protection, etc.) can no longer be financed.[21] As the privatization of public services continues and social expenditure and benefits keep on falling, the question usually directed at the advocates of a basic social income comes to encapsulate the problem of the system as a whole: 'where are you going to get the money from?' Although working time is no longer the measure of created wealth, it still remains the basis for the distribution of incomes and, for the most part, for the sums expended and redistributed by the state. *The trend within the economy is thus for the amounts that are to be levied and redistributed to cover individual and collective needs ultimately to exceed the amounts distributed by and for production.* It is not merely the universal grant of a basic income which cannot be funded on this basis. It is the whole of the state and the society which are coming apart at the seams (something which is very visible in Great Britain and the USA). Wassily Leontief summed up the situation in the following metaphor: 'What would happen if we suddenly found ourselves in [Paradise]? With all goods and services provided without work, no one would be gainfully employed. Being unemployed means receiving no wages. As a result, until appropriate new income policies were formulated to fit the changed technological conditions everyone would starve in Paradise.'[22]

Leontief didn't say precisely what new income policy he had in mind, but Jacques Duboin indicated the 'exit' as early as 1931 and Marx did so in 1857 (in the *Grundrisse*, which Duboin could not have known):[23] *the distribution of means of payment must correspond to the volume of wealth socially produced and not to the volume of work performed.*

As René Passet so succinctly puts it, 'What we regard today as secondary distribution will become primary distribution.' Because it is the product of integrated, 'man–machine–organization' systems in which 'the contribution specific to each person is no longer measurable', 'the national product becomes genuinely collective property . . . The question of distribution is no longer one of commutative, but distributive justice.'[24]

The distribution of means of payment will no longer take the form of a wage, but of what, even in his day, Duboin called a 'social income'. This no longer reflects the 'value' of the labour done (that is to say, of the products necessary to reproduce the labour power expended), but the needs, desires and aspirations society chooses to meet. It requires the creation of another sort of money, which cannot be hoarded and which Passet, following Duboin, calls 'consumption money'.[25]

This is where present developments are heading. They are rendering the 'law of value' obsolete. They require, in fact, a quite different economy in which prices are no longer a reflection of the cost of direct labour contained in the products and the means of labour, a cost which is becoming increasingly marginal, and the price system no longer reflects the exchange-value of products. Prices will necessarily be political prices and the price system will reflect society's choice of a model of consumption and civilization, its choice of a way of life.[26]

When fully thought through, the universal grant of a basic income can be seen as equivalent to a pooling of socially produced wealth. It is a pooling, not a 'sharing out' (the sharing out comes afterwards: you can only share out between everyone what belongs to everyone, what is, at the outset, no one's). René Passet expresses this clearly when he writes of the national product as 'genuinely collective property' produced by collective labour in which it is impossible to assess each person's contribution. As a consequence, the 'from each according to his labour' becomes obsolete. The 'collective worker' is tending to be supplanted by a fundamentally different virtual subject as the direct work of shaping matter is replaced as the main productive force by the 'general state of science . . . or the application of this science to production', that is to say, by the capacity of 'social individuals' to make use of techno-science through their own self-organized co-operation and exchange. It is then 'the free development of individualities' (I am continuing to paraphrase the *Grundrisse* here) by 'the reduction of necessary labour to a minimum', and the production of use-values according to needs, which become the objectives.

The call for a sufficient, universal, unconditional basic income fits in to such a vision. It cannot be achieved immediately, but we must begin to conceptualize it and prepare the way for it as of now. *It has heuristic value: it reflects the most basic and advanced meaning of present developments.* Conversely, it shows up the nonsensical nature of a system which makes unprecedented savings of working time, but turns that time into a disaster for those who save it, because the system can neither share it out, nor share out the produced or producible wealth, nor recognize the intrinsic value of 'leisure and time for higher activities' (Marx). It reveals the way this disposable time is individually and collectively appropriated as a major issue. And it shows the capacity for autonomy – the individual and social ability to make meaningful use of one's disposable time and enjoy it – as a cardinal virtue. It points forward to that other society which can be seen emerging out of present trends.

It is no mere intellectual pastime or self-indulgence to clarify the perspective to which these trends point. It is on such clarification that the capacity to give the most advanced meaning to the changes which are taking place depends. And the capacity also to develop actions, arenas of conflict, and practices which keep that meaning responsive to the latest developments by seeking to take control of those changes. The ultimate goal to which the unconditional grant of a basic income points is that of a society in which the necessity of work is no longer experienced *as such* because each person, from childhood onwards, will be involved in, and feel the attraction of, a general proliferation of artistic, sporting, techno-scientific, artisanal, political, philosophical, ecosophic,[27] relational and co-operative activities all around him/her; a society in which means of production and facilities for self-providing are accessible to everyone at any time of day, just as databanks and teleworking resources already are; in which exchanges are principally exchanges of knowledge, not of commodities, and do not therefore need to be mediated by money; in which the immateriality of the main form of productive work corresponds to the immateriality of the main form of fixed capital. *Once it has been eliminated as a separate, autonomized power,* productive work will consist mainly in the capacity to take advantage of the accumulated knowledge, to enrich and exchange it, *without the valorization of that knowledge imposing itself on individuals as an alien demand,* without it dictating to them the nature, intensity, duration and hours of their work.

It is in this sense that we must understand Marx's remark that 'free time, i.e. time for the full development of the individual . . . from the standpoint of the direct production process . . . can be regarded as the production of fixed capital, this fixed capital being man himself.'[28] In other words, free time enables individuals to develop capacities (of invention, creation, conception and intellection) which give them a virtually unlimited productivity, and this development of their productive capacity, which can be equated with the production of a fixed capital, *is not work,* though it produces the same outcome as work 'from the standpoint of the direct production process'. It is not work, because it was made possible by 'the general reduction of the necessary labour of a society to a minimum'.[29] It is this 'time freed up for their own development' which makes it possible for them to take as their goal 'the free development of individualities', their 'artistic, scientific etc. development'.[30] And it is this free development of individualities which reappears in production as the capacity to create an unlimited variety of wealth with a very small expenditure of time and energy.

In other words, the increase in the productive capacities of individuals is *the consequence, not the goal* of their full development. The goal is not to maximize production for production's sake or power for power's sake – this is the difference between 'man' and 'fixed capital' – but to save on the working time and expenditure of energy *necessary* for achieving a fulfilled life.

'Truly wealthy a nation, when the working day is 6 rather than 12 hours,' wrote an anonymous Ricardian, whom Marx quotes repeatedly, in 1821.[31] It is impossible to state more clearly that *the full development of the productive forces makes the full employment of the productive forces* (in particular, labour power) *unnecessary* and makes it possible for production to become an activity of secondary importance. The 'massive' productivity which techno-science bestows on human labour means that *the maximization of free time, not the maximization of production, becomes the immanent destination and purpose of economic reason.* 'Real economy – saving – consists of the saving of labour time.'[32] 'Real economy' leads to the elimination of work as the dominant form of activity. It is this elimination of work and its replacement by personal activity which we must now make our political goal; it is a goal we can make tangible by achieving changes which are practically attainable as of now.

Redistribution of work, liberation of free time

Companies have been reducing working time and are continuing to do so, month on month. The employers have turned the reduction of working hours into a management tool. Indeed, it has become a method through which companies are coming to have complete control of time, total power over the lives of their workers. The most radical form of this power is the 'zero-hours contract', introduced into Britain by Japanese car firms, and known in Germany as '*Arbeit auf Abruf*'. In this system, the 'employees' are not employed, but are required to be permanently 'on call'. They will then be employed when the company needs them, being paid at the agreed hourly rate for only the few hours or days they work. This marks a return, more or less, to the day-labourers of Dickensian times (though the same scheme currently operates in the docks and in the central markets of some cities), who turned up at the appointed hiring places at dawn in the hope an employer would deign to take them on for a few hours.

The redistribution of work has been effected by dispossessing the workers of any power over their own time: those the firm needs on a permanent basis are employed on flexible terms, depending on the economic situation or the time of year; the others – the temporary, contract, part-time or tele-workers – work intermittently and discontinuously, or not at all. The total annual quantity of work, though it is diminishing, is being spread over an increasing number of workers (statistically, job numbers are rising), in such a way that everyone feels insecure. The employed are fearful of losing their jobs (more than a third of the workforce have already known periods of unemployment in recent years: one out of six has given up looking for a job and no longer figures in the statistics). For around half the workforce (and these people will soon be in the majority), the notions of normal working hours and reduced working time no longer mean anything.

We have to ask what the significance of the 32- or 35-hour week might be, just exactly what it can do for a number of categories of workers, even when converted to an annual basis and with a second cheque added to compensate for the loss of earnings. I am thinking, here, of the person slaving at one McJob after another; 'temping' (in France, half of such assignments are for less than a week; those of four weeks or longer represent only 5.7 per cent of the total); or working half-time for half wages or working spasmodically on a free-lance basis for 75 hours one week in every four or five.

Admittedly, by greatly reducing the weekly (or monthly, or annual) working hours for those in permanent jobs, stable employment can be distributed between more people. The example of Volkswagen has shown this. By reducing the working week from 36 to 28.8 hours, VW initially avoided having to lay off 30,000 workers. However, since this policy was not carried forward, the limits were soon reached. It did not prevent periods of temporary factory close-down, continual shrinkage of the workforce, the introduction of – paid and unpaid – additional holiday periods or new forms of very short hours and discontinuous working.[33]

In short, it showed that a policy of reduction of working time can be effective only if it is an evolving measure, transcending the mere company level. It must take account of the volume of waged work available and the proportion of stable, permanent jobs. If the aim is at the same time to distribute a decreasing quantity of work to an expanding workforce, to increase the proportion of stable, permanent jobs and to offer increased possibilities of workers choosing their own hours, there is only one way open. Work must be made more discontinuous; the workforce must be given a choice between a very wide range of forms of discontinuity, with the result that discontinuity of working can be transformed into a new freedom – *into the right to work intermittently and to lead a multi-active life in which professional work and unpaid activities supplement and complement each other.*

This is what was proposed in France by a medium-sized civil engineering company (Rabot Dutilleul). In the summer of 1996, they introduced the 'one-in-five' system. This allowed members of staff to reduce their working hours by one day, one week or one month in every five. This right to discontinuous working, which is a company policy at Rabot Dutilleul, is a social policy in the Netherlands and Denmark, a blueprint for society. All imaginable forms of reduced working arrangements are to be found in the Netherlands, where there is the highest percentage of part-time workers in the world (37 per cent). The main Dutch trade union (FNV) has published a ten-point guide entitled 'Choose your working hours for yourself.' From the two-, three- or four-day week to the four-, six- or nine-month year, all possible combinations and options are available.

The Danes brought in a law in 1993 which takes them even further down this same path. They variously employ systems of 'one in four', 'one in seven' (sabbatical year) or 'one in ten', with a corresponding increase in the numbers of permanent staff. This law is in fact a highly flexible variant of the scheme Michel Albert proposed in his 1982 book, *Le Pari français*.[34] It allows any employee to take a year's leave, which may be broken up and divided out in any way he/she wishes over a period of his/her choice. During the period of leave, unemployed persons will take the place of the employees on voluntary leave, who, for their part, will receive 70 per cent of the unemployment benefit they would get if they were to lose their jobs. That benefit usually amounts to 90 per cent of final salary for up to five years.

Though this right was initially conceived as an individual one, the trade unions have managed to use it imaginatively to reduce the working hours of entire company workforces and to increase the number of permanent jobs. In one case, public transport workers decided to increase their staffing level by 10 per cent by organizing in such a way that one-tenth of them were always on leave. The Aarhus refuse collectors organized themselves to increase their workforce by 25 per cent. They increased the teams on each refuse lorry to a nominal figure of four, but each employee only works three weeks out of four. This involves a 9 per cent loss of earnings for a 25 per cent reduction in working hours.

These various schemes show that discontinuity of work does not necessarily mean greater employment insecurity. Indeed, the more discontinuous the work, the greater the security of employment can be, as discontinuous working is in the end merely a reduction in monthly, annual or pluri-annual working hours, with the work being spread out over a greater number of people. The right to a sabbatical year every five, seven or ten years; the right to training leave every year or every few years; the right to a year of parental leave, which the two parents can share, divide up as they wish and spread over three years following the birth of a child (the Swedish scheme); the right to take leave to care for a sick child or relative; the right, which exists only in embryonic form (for trade-union officials and representatives, for example), to take leave for activities of general utility – all this leads to making professional activity increasingly intermittent and has, in the end, the same effect as work sharing. The same task or function is shared by several persons who hand on to each other and all have other interests and activities in their lives.

A flexible workforce can mean something other than insecurity of employment and recourse to temporary and contract workers, who are hired and fired as the order book fills and empties. Flexibility can mean increasing or decreasing the discontinuity of work, as in the Danish system; it can mean increasing or reducing the proportion of people who can take leave at the same time, while retaining their status and job security.

It is, therefore, possible to rethink discontinuous working, to rethink the flexibility of working hours and staffing as a source not of insecurity, but of security, and as a form of the right to 'choose one's own working hours'. This makes it possible to reduce the comparative importance of employment in everyone's life and to give those who want it the chance to vary their work, change companies, keep on the move, experience new ways of living and new activities. *All the forms of passively suffered discontinuity of employment, passively suffered flexibility of working hours and staffing levels, should be transformed into opportunities to choose and self-manage discontinuity and flexibility.*

The Danish system is currently the one offering the greatest scope in this regard. Instead of subsidizing employment to reduce wage costs, it subsidizes non-work and increases the workers' power in terms of the self-organization and self-management of their mode of co-operation. The principles of this system contain in embryo the outlines of a different society and economy:

1   It recognizes that the right to work and the right not to work are of equal importance and are indissociably linked. The former cannot exist without the latter. The ideology of work is discouraged, while the idea of work sharing is promoted.
2   It recognizes everyone's right to work discontinuously, while also recognizing the right to a continuous income. This latter

is not an unemployment benefit, since unemployment is not in this case (as its legal definition stipulates) an absence of work *passively suffered* by the unemployed person, but an interruption of work which he/she has *chosen*, and been encouraged to choose by a legal provision. That choice is legitimated politically in so far as it chimes in with a particular political option, a new blueprint for society. The allowance paid to the 'voluntary unemployed' is 63 per cent of their normal wage (not 63 per cent of the minimum wage), which lifts the income of a half-time worker to 81.5 per cent of the full-time rate and that of a quarter-time worker to 72.25 per cent of full-time. The allowance is, in reality, a guaranteed social income.

3   This system can be applied with very great flexibility in both large and small companies. In tiny craft-based companies or in the case of sole traders – where the working week most often exceeds 48 hours – it will tend to take the form of job sharing or the formation of co-operative links between several craftspeople, pooling their jobs and orders.

In this arrangement, discontinuity of work is no longer synonymous with insecurity. The more intermittent work is, the easier it is to ensure security of employment. The workforce also have greater freedom to choose their hours and periods of work. Conversely, the more the quantity of socially necessary labour time diminishes, the more discontinuous, when it is distributed among everyone, will work necessarily become.

But this is where we run up against the limitations of the Danish system. It guarantees everyone a *conditional* social income during his/her periods away from employment. It cannot, however, guarantee that everyone can meet the conditions which entitle workers to that social income, unless it were to put a constantly reducing figure on the period of employment by which workers qualify for leave. As the quantity of socially necessary labour diminishes, periods away from employment will tend to become longer than periods spent in employment, activities performed for oneself will tend to assume greater significance than paid work, and the social income will tend to become larger than the salary.[35] The social income will become less and less conditional in nature and will increasingly have to become something like an unconditional, universal grant.

None the less, the 'continuous income for discontinuous working' formula – in which the discontinuity can be managed by work collectives – is particularly interesting as a 'transitional policy'. It is a policy which is evolutionary and highly unstable, and one which pre-empts a funding crisis that will raise the question of redefining the basic principles and forms of the welfare state and the basic orientations of the economy and society. By the high degree of self-organization, consultation and solidarity it generates among workers, it prepares the ground for the basic conflict that will emerge as the welfare system enters into crisis.

Changing work

I am well aware that anyone who speaks of guaranteeing a sufficient social income ends up hearing the following objection: 'It will greatly weaken the incentive to work and society will end up short of labour.' There is no good counter-argument to this objection. The only appropriate reply is 'We have to see to it that this problem does not arise.' We have to see to it that there is no need for 'incentives' (which are, in fact, constraints) for people to want to work. Dominique Méda has shown up the contradiction in the 'dominant social discourse' very clearly.[36] It presents 'work' as a fundamental human need, as an indispensable 'social bond', a virtue, the main source of self-esteem and the esteem of others, but as soon as there is mention of social rights not being linked to work, the danger of 'weakening the incentive to work' rears its head. So 'work' isn't actually so attractive, gratifying, satisfying or integrating that you don't need to give people 'incentives' by setting benefit rates for the unemployed at a level below subsistence income.

In short (I shall come back to this point at greater length in the next chapter), to change society, we have to change 'work' – and vice versa. To change it by divesting it of all its reifying constraints (hours, hierarchy, productivity), which reflect its subordination to capital and which, so far, have determined the essence of what is currently known as 'work'. To change it by reconciling it with a culture of daily life, an art of living, which it would both extend and nourish, instead of being cut off from them.[37] To change it by the way it will be *appropriated* from childhood onwards, when it will be possible no longer to suffer it as a penance, but to live it as an activity merged in the flow of life, a path to the full development of the senses, towards power over oneself and the external world, and as a bond with others. To change it from childhood onwards by linking the acquisition of knowledge with a pride in being able to do things (this was a conception already developed by Blonski, among others, at the end of the nineteenth century). It is not hard to imagine considerable advances in this direction by combining (self-)teaching with group ecological, social and cultural projects. Work, study, experiment, exchange, artistic practice and personal fulfilment would all go hand in hand here, with people quite naturally being accorded a basic income at the end of adolescence.[38]

We might envisage this income, which would at first be partial, becoming a full one as the adolescents acquired and developed ranges of competence by taking on practical tasks of increasing diversity, complexity and skill, in community activities – and particularly in the public services – alongside their 'studies'. 'Work' might then become quite naturally one of the dimensions of life, accompanied by and alternating with a range of other activities in which 'productivity' is not a consideration, though those activities would contribute indirectly to the productivity of labour by way of the creative, imaginative and expressive capacities they developed.

Rainer Zoll recently proposed a transitional formula for moving in this direction. As they reach the end of adolescence, citizens could each sign up for a variable period in a voluntary civilian service offering a choice from a wide range of activities of an ecological, social or cultural nature. This service – *which would bestow greater social respect for being voluntary* – 'the productivity of which would not be measurable in economic terms' and which, as a consequence, 'must not be regarded as commodity labour to be remunerated with a wage', would allow considerable scope for initiative on the part of the volunteers in determining their tasks and their hours. It would entitle the volunteers to a 'citizenship income', providing them with a 'normal standard of living' not just during their period of service but for a period two or three times its length: 'For example, two or three years' service would entitle the volunteers to four or five more years' social income, without any other obligation on their part.'[39]

Zoll's prescription can be seen as a variant of the Danish scheme. Like the latter, it proposes a conditional social income linked to a *period* of work, without claiming to be able to measure the corresponding *quantity* of work. One might envisage a scheme in which such periods of voluntary service were repeated throughout a person's working life; in which some public services would operate with voluntary labour; and in which bonuses were added to the basic social income to reflect the experience and qualifications of the volunteer, and the length and intensity of his/her involvement.

Changing the city

We have to see the guarantee of a basic social income and the expansion of disposable time not as something which would reduce activity, but as a way of increasing it. Their purpose is not to exempt people from doing anything at all, but to open up possibilities for everyone to engage in a whole host of individual or collective, private or public activities – activities which no longer need to be profitable in order to flourish. From childhood onwards, everyone is to be involved in, and feel the attraction of, a general proliferation of groups, teams, workshops, clubs, co-operatives, associations and networks, all seeking to recruit him/her into their activities and projects. Artistic, political, scientific, ecosophic, sporting, craft and relational activities; self-providing, work on repairing and restoring the natural and cultural heritage, improving the environment, energy saving; crèches, 'health shops', networks for the exchange of services, for mutual aid and assistance, etc.

These self-activities, which are self-organized, self-managed, voluntary and open to everyone, must not be perceived as lamely supplementing the capitalist market economy, nor as an obligatory *quid pro quo* for the basic income which makes them possible. With no need of capital, no need to valorize capital and certainly no need that the wants and desires they aim to satisfy be backed by money, they may be called on to take the social time and space which the reduction in the volume of work frees up out of capitalist, market logic. They may be called on, too, to supplant wage-working to a very large extent and to create, beyond that form, free, associative social bonds; to become hegemonic and, to that end, to be spaces of resistance to the powers that be, spaces for experiment, for mounting a practical challenge to our crumbling society, for developing alternative socialities, and social alternatives to that society.

Urban policy can give a decisive boost to this ferment of varied self-activity, in which the project for a new and different society can begin to take shape and become aware of itself. Through the organization of space and social time, through the facilities, amenities and sites it puts at their disposal, urban policy calls upon people to develop these activities, provides them with the resources they need, confirms them as the kinds of activity a society struggling to emerge expects from everyone. It reflects them back to themselves not as ephemeral improvisations or tame palliatives adopted for want of something better, but as a common endeavour in which all may share, a project in which new social relations are to be developed.

Where policies on time and cities are concerned, many useful ideas have been developed in the Netherlands and Denmark. Why do 37 per cent of the Dutch – 70 per cent of women and more than 17 per cent of men – opt to work part-time, even though their wages are reduced proportionately, without any compensation? Why do 22 per cent of the men still working full-time want to change to part-time, even if it means earning less, whereas only 4 per cent of women and men working part-time want to work longer? Why is it that in their eyes the use-value of the time spent not working is greater than the exchange-value of the time spent doing paid work (i.e. than the extra money they could earn)?

We might guess that the density of the urban fabric has a lot to do with it, and that the layout of towns and cities, the architecture, the collective amenities and public transport are designed in such a way as to facilitate self-activity, interaction, creation and co-operation. Herbert Marcuse was fond of saying, 'After the revolution, we shall tear down the cities and rebuild them.' By changing towns and cities, we shall provide a lever for social change and for a change in the way people relate to one another and live out their essential belonging to the world. The reconstitution of a liveable life-world presupposes clearly laid-out, polycentric towns and cities, in which each district or neighbourhood offers a range of sites accessible to everyone at any time for self-activities, self-providing, self-directed learning, exchanges of services and knowledge; a profusion of day nurseries, parks, meeting places, sports grounds, gymnasiums, workshops, music rooms, schools, theatres and libraries; dwelling-houses with meeting places and walkways, play areas for children, restaurant/kitchens for the old or the disabled, etc.

There are many of these features in the model which the town of Parthenay has been developing since the early 1980s.[40] In

Copenhagen and Bologna, too, many such aspects are present. Félix Guattari writes that:

> New modes of domestic life, new practices of neighbourliness, education, culture, sport, childcare, care for the elderly and the sick . . . are within our grasp, as are new social values and a new style of activity. The only thing missing is the desire and the political resolve to take on such changes . . .
>
> Will we have to wait for overall political changes before undertaking 'molecular revolutions' of this kind, which are to contribute to changing mentalities? We are in a cleft stick here: on the one hand, society, politics and the economy can evolve only if there is a change of mentalities, whilst, on the other, mentalities cannot really change unless society as a whole undergoes change. The large-scale social experimentation we advocate will be one of the ways out of that contradiction. A few successful experiments in creating new living spaces would have significant consequences in stimulating a general resolve for change . . .
>
> The point is to construct something . . . providing every opportunity for the potential mutations which will lead coming generations to live, feel and think differently. The quality of the production of this new subjectivity should become the primary goal of human activities.[41]

In fact, as we saw in chapter 3, mentalities or, rather, sensibilities are already changing, and with them the system of values. But this cultural change remains a personal, private matter for each individual, so long as it is not translated into a new organization of social space moulded by that change and allowing it to express itself, to be objectified in new ways of acting and living in society. It is a matter of changing towns and cities so that the 'new subjectivity' is no longer merely a change in 'my head' or 'my heart' – a change which the dominant social discourse denies or represses – so that this change can be embodied in the material world, in practices and discourses, can develop a dynamic which carries it beyond its initial intentions and turns it into a common project, into the 'general will'.

Local Exchange Trading Systems (LETS)

As both a crisis measure and a source of 'new subjectivity', Local Exchange Trading Systems (LETS) are among the best examples of large-scale social experimentation. They represent an 'exodus' from present social arrangements, producing new socialities beyond the power of the state and money. LETS were invented during the 1920s in Germany and developed in various forms in the USA during the great depression of the 1930s. Since the end of the eighties, they have been spreading in a new form in Europe, North America and Australia. They are called *Systèmes d'échange locaux* (SELs) in France and *Kooperationsringe* (co-operative circles) in Germany, but the most dynamic expansion has been in Great Britain, largely thanks to the efforts of Michael Linton, the founder of Manchester LETS.[42]

LETS or co-operative circles (circle being a much more appropriate title than 'system') are a potentially radical response to the impossibility, as a result of unemployment, for large masses of workers of *selling* their labour power. They respond to this situation by putting economic exchange on a quite different footing. To sell their labour power for money, workers need an 'employer' capable of paying them and selling on the labour 'employed' to a customer who is able to pay for it. But why should labour always be 'employed' by someone who does not perform it? Why should it always pass through the commodity form – and hence through money – to be exchanged, recognized, valued? Why shouldn't the members of a community exchange their work without intermediaries, 'in the most rational and human way possible' (Marx), by tailoring the goods and services produced as directly as possible to needs and desires which are themselves expressed without any intermediary?

The question is as old as the labour movement and unemployment, and the workers' movement has always attempted to find a solution by eliminating the intermediaries who come between the workers and their products, and then between those products and those who need them. But that elimination has many disadvantages if it merely means reverting to payments in kind – a return to barter. For barter has to be done 'on the spot', one thing being exchanged for another. It permits only of specific, determinate exchange between two determinate persons who, unless they know each other well, do not afford each other credit.

The Local Exchange Trading System or co-operative circle eliminates these disadvantages by creating a work-money or time-money which makes it possible to exchange any service or product against any other. In this it resembles money, though it is not money and has none of its powers. This is the revolutionary aspect of the formula.

The founding principle of a circle is that everyone is 'solvent', since everyone has capacities, skills or talents which others may need. They may, moreover, develop those skills and acquire others if given the opportunity. It is with this 'immaterial capital' that they join a 'co-operative circle'. This begins by granting them credit and they may call on the services of other members as and when they need them. Every hour of work – or its equivalent – which they receive from a member represents a debt they will have to pay off within a certain period (most often between three months and one year) by an hour of work for any of the other members of the network. The co-operative circle is, therefore, a mutualist network, based on what Claus Offe and Rolf Heinze accurately refer to as 'serial reciprocity'.[43]

From the outset, co-operative circles took from the co-operative movement the principle of the equality of their members, and of the equivalence and equal dignity of their members' work. Every hour worked entitles one to receive an hour's work in return, or its equivalent, while every hour of work received represents a debt of one hour.[44] A computer record of each member's current balance is easy to maintain, that balance being expressed in time-money ('time dollars' in the USA) with the unit of time most often being the hour.

Unlike official money, however, time-money or work-money has a short life and is limited in its convertibility: it has currency only within the issuing circle (though the possible networking of several circles is under discussion in Britain) and it loses its value if it is not 'spent' within three or six months, depending on the period set. It must not, then, be hoarded. It must not allow some, by doing work without ever asking for anything in return, to achieve a position of almost unlimited credit over all the others and in that way – like bankers or professional lenders – to acquire dominance.

Unlike the British labour exchanges of the nineteenth century, which were based on the direct exchange of labour, co-operative circles do not, therefore, abolish money, nor even the market. They do, however, abolish *the power of money*, the blind 'law of the market', and they make that market transparent. Given its short life, the local money issued by a circle cannot be desired for its own sake. It cannot serve to enrich some and impoverish others, nor can it play a part in capitalist investment for profit. It cannot be used for the privative appropriation of the wealth of the community. It limits private property and each person's purchasing power to what he/she may take for 'the use of [his/her] Family and a plentiful supply to its Consumption' (Locke), whilst money, by enabling some to enrich themselves, enables the rich man to possess 'more . . . than he himself can use the product of'.[45]

The short 'life' of local money thus encourages spending and self-restraint at one and the same time. It provides an incentive for all members of the scheme to put back into circulation the time-credit they have acquired through their work, by themselves requesting services from other members. But it also encourages everyone to limit their consumption of other people's labour since they will have to settle their debts within a limited time by providing services themselves. Since it links all acquisition and consumption to an expenditure of work and time, local money abolishes the fetishism of money (the appearance that whatever anyone can do, money can do it better) and commodity fetishism, stimulates reflection on the reality of needs and discourages waste. Its watchword could be 'to each according to their needs, to each according to their work'.

Yet a third aspect explains political ecology's interest in co-operative circles: local money encourages greater use of local resources, products and services. Since it is exchangeable only within a limited area, it boosts and develops the local economy, increases the degree of self-sufficiency and the power the population can exert on economic orientations and priorities. It spurs people to prioritize the creation of use-values over the production of exchange-values. The more members and varied skills a co-operative circle has, the greater the proportion of trade it will be possible to transact in local money, and this will tend to replace the official money. For example, in El Paso (New Mexico) you can pay doctor's fees in time dollars; in Ithaca (New York) most shopkeepers take 'green money'; in certain Dutch towns, restaurants take the local money, as do some banks in Britain.

A Swedish researcher, Nordal Åkerman, who was one of the first in Europe to take an interest in the eco-socially transformative potential of co-operative circles, saw them as a means to 'shrink the size of units in society and to make people active and in command of the development'. He proposed linking the entire population in every area with the co-operative movement by drawing up a list of the needs which could be covered by local production – beginning with needs for water, heating, foodstuffs, transport, basic textiles, machines and waste disposal. He also suggested drawing up 'a list of all those small things that would help to make life in the local communities more active, rewarding and pleasant. This could be done through local referendums where people would be asked to make a choice of some 20–30 items and have the possibility of adding five to ten of their own suggestions.'[46]

The co-operative circle must not be conceived, then, as an isolated measure, for the use of the unemployed and the marginalized. If this were the case, it would merely be papering over the cracks in the system, and its local money would be seen from the outset as 'paupers' money'. Moreover, the services reciprocally provided would be seen as gimmicks for 'keeping a lid on trouble spots', and dismantling and privatizing public services and welfare provision.

And co-operative circles must also not be seen as attempts to get back to the village economy. In fact, they will be at their most developed in a context where everyone is unconditionally guaranteed a basic income, where everyone 'works' intermittently in the system of macro-social exchange, acquiring, maintaining and developing within that system skills which can also be used and traded at the micro-social level, particularly in the local, co-operative production of goods and services for local consumption. It is then conceivable that the co-operators may club together to buy or hire high-performance equipment or the parts and components to build such equipment themselves. It is also conceivable that the productivity of local self-providing activities – and also their quality – may be comparable or superior to that of existing large firms. Conceivable too that the skill levels and degree of inventiveness of local teams may, thanks to the continual interchange of ideas and competences and the intensity of communication and co-operation, exceed the level met in industry.

On all these points, the initiatives of the Center for New Work founded by Frithjof Bergmann have provided practical confirmation which I did not expect to meet so soon.[47]

The viability of a co-operative circle and its development depend to a large extent on the speed with which it takes off. This in turn depends on the logistical support its founders are given by the local authority. A number of left local authorities in Britain have created LETS development officers to aid this process. This has largely involved providing premises for LETS groups, and also workshops, means of production, computer equipment, technical advice, training and learning opportunities and so on.

The spread of computerization gives a constant boost to the potential of co-operative networks. Computers can be used to make their management transparent and easy to monitor by all the members. It is possible now for all the services offered and requested, times of availability, and members' balances to be displayed permanently on the Internet. This reduces, and may even eliminate, the economies of scale by which in the past large-scale commercial production swept aside local production and domestic self-providing. It makes self-teaching and self-directed learning easier, and facilitates possible co-ordination, specialization and exchanges between networks, which could, for example, pool their resources to acquire more technically advanced equipment than would be within the reach of a single network of just a few hundred members.

The co-operative circle may thus lead gradually to *the collective appropriation of the new technologies*, including, Claus Haeffner suggests, flexible computerized manufacturing systems which would be acquired by the local authority on a hire-purchase basis, or which its members would 'put together', in much the same way as computer and mechanical equipment is recovered in the shanty towns of Africa or South America and 'cannibalized' to meet local needs.[48] There is now no longer any great gulf between the performance of the brand-marked production tools of industry and the tools a local community can use for self-producing, after having produced those tools themselves at a price which seems laughable by comparison with that of branded products. In so far as such a gulf still does potentially exist, it is (more than) compensated for by the greater satisfaction the members of a circle derive from their co-operative practice.

'Social-technocratic professionalization', as Offe and Heinze call it, has discredited and suppressed vernacular skills and disqualified people's capacity to take care of themselves, judge for themselves, help each other and communicate.[49] Co-operative circles make it possible to take back into the sphere of neighbourly relations at least some of the services on which professional social services claim a monopoly. Offe and Heinze cite the example of home care for the temporarily disabled. But the short-term validity of local monies puts those services which need to be provided reliably day after day for months or years, for people who cannot provide equivalent services in return within the required time scale, beyond the scope of a circle. This is the case, for example, with mothers' help services and home help for the permanently disabled or the aged. Hence the idea, summed up in the slogan 'from welfare state to welfare society', of a social insurance system based on contributions of services rendered rather than money. Fit pensioners could commit themselves to giving regular assistance and care to the needy and thereby build up a credit balance which they could draw on when they themselves need care and assistance, wherever they are. Or the relatives of people with care needs could pass on to them time-credits they have acquired for this purpose. The result would be greater autonomy for the persons in need of care. They would no longer need to call on the goodwill and, most importantly, the availability of the members of their family.

Such a system would clearly be of little value or advantage if it depended on 'obligatory volunteering' and were aimed at dismantling social services and their public provision. Its goal must be to keep people involved throughout their lives in the network of social intercourse. The social value of co-operative circles does not lie simply in the creation of 'utilities' which could not otherwise have been produced and traded. It lies just as much in the demonstration that, apart from money, there are other – more concrete and convivial – currencies, sources of rights and accounting units. It lies in establishing relations of fair, stable and continuous reciprocity, which offer a haven from insecurity and uncertainty. It lies, as Jessen noted, in the self-determination of the services rendered and received and in the non-hierarchical character of the social relations of co-operation and exchange. These 'sustain individuals' critical consciousness and their dignity' and, unlike paid work, 'are experienced as free and unalienated', as 'communicative relations exempt from domination'. All of which are apt to reinforce in individuals a critical and militantly proactive attitude in respect of the organization and quality of work within the capitalist company.[50]

Reverting to the political

This brings us right back to the heart of our subject. In the co-operative circles and the potential networking of those circles, we see the beginnings of a practical critique of the job system. Each circle is a collective whose members themselves take control of work and its distribution, together with the specification, acquisition and diffusion of knowledge, skills and techniques. Or they have, at least, the potential to do this. This is a large-scale social experiment which may offer those taking part an intimation of a different society and economy, in which wage-labour, the power of money and the supremacy of 'market laws' (though not markets themselves) are abolished. They may obtain a glimpse of a society and an economy freed from the rule of 'real abstraction', where it will no longer be true to say that 'it doesn't matter what your work is, so long as you have a job.'

As the field of their co-operation expands, will the 'associated producers' in the circles still accept the constraints and limits set on their self-organization and associative co-operation by the capitalist organization of work, even when it takes the Toyotist form? Will they still be willing to subordinate their capacities and skills to capital? Will they, to 'earn a living', still continue to serve alien goals when, by the transnational strategies of deterritorialized decision-makers, they are denied the right to examine these critically – or even to know what they are? Will they still allow economic and technological decisions to be made without public debate, or permit the state and/or capital to exert their 'dictatorship over needs' and over the model of consumption? Won't 'critical consciousness', fortified by a practice of co-operation which is itself a practical critique, spill over from the circles and invade companies, administrative authorities, political apparatuses? Won't the capacity to *produce* science, and not just apply it, lead to an increasingly radical challenge to the mandarins and the institutions and industries that confiscate science and research for their own benefit – a challenge which is already seen in the self-help networks set up by cancer, diabetes and AIDS patients, or drug-users, or in the consumer and ecology movements? These too, it may be noted, are often transnational in nature.

I shall not venture to speculate here on the path this kind of revolution may take, nor the possible links and mediations between the local, micro-social sphere of co-operative communities and the macro-society in which they remain immersed. It is impossible to separate them theoretically and practically from the space which is common to all of them, which connects them together and provides for what they cannot achieve on their own. We have to accept that the problem of their relation to that space – which is nothing but society itself, opened on to the world – does arise; that there is a need for, and a problem of, mediations between each local community and society in general, and between communities themselves and societies themselves; that that problem and those mediations are *the problems of the political* and of politics, which will not be made magically to fade away by communicative, consensual relations between local communities. We must accept that the village community cannot be extended to planetary scale – and neither can the self-managed co-operative. We must accept that the wealth of a society and a civilization also depend on the existence of *large* territorial collectivities, of cities which are large enough for highly specialized and minority activities to exist in them – for the existence of cellists and Egyptologists, micro-surgeons and astrophysicists, psychotherapists and judo teachers, etc. And it depends too on the existence of large-scale bodies and public services, such as universities and research institutes, museums and shipyards, etc. And all this presupposes that society will produce an accumulable 'economic surplus', and that there will, therefore, be money functioning as a universal equivalent, known and accepted rules applicable to all, and consequently a legal code and system, an organ of co-ordination and equalization, in short, *the thing we call a state.*[51]

The 'system' cannot dissolve itself entirely into the 'life-world', says Habermas. This means the public services and administrations of complex modern societies cannot dissolve themselves entirely into the communicative and consensual co-operation between communities. It is, however, possible for productive co-operation and self-organized social exchanges increasingly to take on a political dimension, through which the insertion of local activities into their wider context can be managed, so that the micro-social ensembles can themselves assume a growing proportion of their mediations with the social whole and become actors in macro-social decisions, which will then come under pressure to link in with micro-social activities. It is at this kind of feedback loop, connecting the evolution of the system back to that of the life-world, each spurring on the other, that Rainer Land has worked constantly, developing, among other things, the model for a politics of ecological restructuring.[52]

This two-way feedback leads – and indeed obliges – micro-social ensembles to think out their own goals as local expressions of universal aims, and to see their 'local common good' as the particular local form of the 'general common good'. The political mediation is, in the last instance, merely the never-finished work of seeking to promote the universal, to express needs in terms of political rights, while rendering the needs of each individual consonant with the needs of all, and vice versa.[53]

Epilogue

It will have taken twenty-five wasted years for the prospect of an increasingly rapid contraction in the volume of necessary 'work' – and hence a possible and desirable reduction in the number of hours' work provided by each of us – to be taken seriously in France. Twenty years have been wasted since the Adret collective gave a voice to the blue- and white-collar workers who had chosen multi-activity, self-activity and reduced working hours and who experienced these things as a liberation.[1] More than twenty years have been wasted since Michel Rolant propounded the slogan that 'less work for every-one means work for all and a better life'. More than twenty-five years have been wasted since the head of IG Metall's automation section, Günther Friedrich, demonstrated that investment no longer creates jobs, but actually eliminates them – unless working hours are con-stantly reduced – and that everything has to be re-examined, rethought and redefined from the bottom up, beginning with the practice, aims and content of trade unionism.

For twenty-five years, Western societies have been reversing into the future, incapable either of reproducing themselves in accordance with past norms or of exploiting the unprecedented freedom of choice made possible by savings in working time. Over those twenty or so years, the societies produced by Fordism have been falling apart without any other form of society establishing itself. They have fallen apart and been replaced by non-societies, in which a tiny dominant stratum has grabbed almost all the additional wealth which has become available, whilst the absence of political bearings and of a political project has led to the dissolution of all social ties, to a hatred of everything, including hatred of life and self.

I don't know if my way of attempting to liberate desires or to unfetter imaginations will have been the right one. Nor do I know if policies on the lines I have sketched out will ever be followed. To those who reject them out of hand as a 'utopia', I say only that it is the function of utopias, in the sense the term has assumed in the work of Ernst Bloch or Paul Ricoeur, to provide us with the distance from the existing state of affairs which allows us to judge what we *are* doing in the light of what we *could* or *should* do. On the other hand, I know we haven't got twenty years to make up for our past failings. The fact is that what is being established all around us is a utopia in the etymological sense of the term: a kind of real unreality super-added to the ruins of a defunct world, weaving around us a secondary, so-called 'virtual' world in which time, place, depth and resistance have no meaning; in which everyone is everywhere – and consequently nowhere – all the time; in which each place is an 'anywhere' interchangeable with all others; and everyone has a place which, whatever it may be, is never their own. U-topia: a dematerialized, decentred world, alienated from the rhythms of the body and from the need of the senses to construct themselves by constructing, in a labour which remains forever unfinished, a reality which opposes those senses and resists them.

The digitalization of everything does not simply abolish work (in the sense of *poiesis*) and the intelligence of hand and body. It abolishes the sensible world, renders the sensory faculties redundant, denies them the capacity to judge between true and false, good and bad. It disqualifies the senses, steals perception's certainties away, takes the ground from under our feet. Increasingly effective artificial aids are replacing the sense organs; technical implants are invading and colonizing the body itself, motorizing it. Electronic stimulation has been substituted for the stimuli of the tangible world. That stimulation provides the body with more intense thrills than the perceptual faculties, which have become irrelevant, and over-compensates in hallucinatory mode for the absence of sensible reality.

The sensibility of living beings has been overlaid with the self-programmable delirium of the cyborg, rejecting as obsolete the natural form of the body which prevents one from having 'cosmic sensations'. By disqualifying manual intelligence and the work of the senses, techno-science abolishes and disqualifies what Günther Anders called 'the humanity of humanity'.[2] The writings of Paul Virilio on this subject are path-breaking, and I confine myself to paraphrasing them here.[3]

The boundaries between technology and biology, between machines and humanity, have been broken down; we see the cybernetic monopolization of sensual pleasure; the reinvention of the body by the re-engineering of its organic architecture, with molecular micro-machines and protein engines capable of self-repair and self-reproduction, able to make 'limitless quantities of food or endless quantities of housing for the homeless, and to move around in arteries to repair cells'.[4] We shall have buildings reaching thousands of metres into the sky and the hundreds of thousands of tenants living in them, in bubbles, like pioneers to distant planets, will never set foot on the ground: 'The dynamic of techno-science is tending to become a kind of autonomous movement beyond people's control', bringing with it the loss of their own world and their own bodies. 'It is as though the accumulation of material – and immaterial – goods revealed itself to be an immense machine for subordinating and conditioning the agents of consumption and production. The external (and perverse) effects end up externalizing those who produced them in the first place.'[5]

What does it mean, in these conditions, to 'take back techno-science'? Who can take it back? What subject could lay hold of it? The question becomes a fundamental one, the central issue in a fundamental conflict, when techno-science ceases to be the product of human praxis and substitutes itself for human praxis, turning men and women into 'the product of their product' (to a degree which could not have been imagined when Marx coined the formula). By acquiring autonomy from its inventors, this product, techno-science, becomes the quasi-subject of production, thought and development. It gains the power not only to produce products, goods or services, not only to produce its consumers, but to *produce its own producers*, to abolish the frontier between the technical and the living, between machine thought and machine language, on the one hand, and the language properly so called of living subjects, on the other. 'Technosophia', for which 'life is technology' and vice versa, says just this. In other words, the subject is technology, and bioengineering, mental engineering usher in the reign of a trans-human, supra-human subject inconceivable to human beings, which rethinks, redesigns and recreates them by laying hold of them body and soul.[6]

What technosophia and the cyborg cult interpret as accession to the cosmic power of a superhuman freed from weaknesses and finitude can more truthfully be interpreted as a total victory of capital which, by becoming immaterial, succeeds in expropriating human beings from their bodies and their worlds to take total possession of their lives. Just as the boundary between the technical and the living is fading, so is the difference between human beings and capital. Marx's formulation, 'from the point of view of the direct production process the full development of the individual is a production of fixed capital, that fixed capital being man himself', is degraded to an absolute productivism in which 'man himself' no longer exists as a productive force and no longer pursues 'the full development of his individuality' as an end in itself, but as a means of increasing his productive power. In pursuing the abolition of work, capital is pursuing the abolition of 'man himself' to subsume or absorb him into itself, to make him *its* subject. Those who remember the essays in which François George, writing as Daniel Verrès, demonstrated that capital functions ontologically as *ens causa sui*, or, in other words, as God, will realize that this interpretation has philosophical as well as intuitive evidence on its side.[7]

It clearly shows where the conflict lies and what is at issue in that conflict: the fault line runs through every sphere in which the right of persons over themselves, over their lives, over their capacity to produce themselves and understand themselves as subjects is in question. It is wherever their right to give meaning to their lives is at stake, and their right to resist everything and everyone that dispossesses them of their meaning, their bodies, their common culture – that deprives them of a place where they can feel 'at home' and where acting and thinking, imagination and action can flourish in unison.

I shall come back to this question shortly in a long commentary on *Critique of Modernity*, among other works, by Alain Touraine, a book which is, in many respects, what Max Weber termed a *Zeitdiagnose*, the quasi-clinical portrait of a disparate world whose scattered fragments have no organizing principle to unify them. The impossibility of such unification is something I have been constantly aware of throughout this work; it is a point which communitarianism obtusely denies. This is why, before turning to Touraine's *Zeitdiagnose*, I include the following digression on the distinction between community and society, cultural identity and citizenship, life-world and subject: in short, the distinction between the community I have been writing of – based on self-organized co-operation and pooling of resources – and the community, exclusive and cohesive in its thinking, which one is supposed, according to most communitarians, to belong to 'constitutively'.

Digression 1
Community and Society

In sociology, the term 'community' usually refers to a grouping or collective whose members are linked, as concrete persons, by a concrete, lived solidarity. The community between these persons has a factual basis: it rests on something each feels he/she has in common with all the other members. This is either something they have *chosen* to have in common, regarding it as their common interest, concern or endeavour – in which case we speak of an associative or co-operative community – or something they have in common originally and by birth – their language, culture, 'country' or *Heimat* – in which case we speak of an originary or 'constitutive' community.

In neither case is the bond between the members of a community a juridical one, or one that is officially established, formalized or otherwise institutionally guaranteed. Nor is it contractual. It is a lived, existential bond, which loses its communal quality the moment it is institutionalized or codified, since, if it were institutionalized, it would acquire an independent objective existence that would no longer need the affective investment and lived commitment of all the members to keep it in being. It is precisely the function of institutionalization to sustain a bond whether or not each member maintains his/her affective commitment. This transforms lived adherence into determinate obligations. A common form of life and shared practices, regulated 'communicatively' and intuitively, give way to a practice governed by juridical rules.

Society, by contrast, is too large, differentiated and complex for the relations between its 'members' to be regulated communicatively and spontaneously. One does not belong to a society, then, in the same way as one belongs to a community. One belongs to it not as a concrete person, having, by one's origin or through co-operation, a shared life with the others, but as a citizen; that is to say, as an abstract person defined in one's universality by established, juridically formalized rights (and duties), guaranteed by a state. The citizen is not the subject-person him/herself, but only the person juridically defined in his/her universality. Between citizens there is no concrete community and immediate lived solidarity, but simply a 'political community . . . detaching the universality of the person from the empirical contexts', and conferring on that universality 'a political identity which is not based on a cultural one' – at least in non-totalitarian societies.[1] Modern society – what Serge Latouche calls *'la grande société'*,[2] as opposed to tribal societies – is thus the antithesis of community: it is the 'loss or disintegration of communal intimacy', the 'dissolution of the old communities . . . through the birth of the nation-state'.[3] In other words, it is the substitution of juridical relations between emancipated individuals for communal bonds based on a traditional *order* which assigns each person his/her place and governs all aspects of daily life, including relations between man and wife or parents and children. In such an order, the distinction between the public and private spheres does not exist.

The *'grande société'* thus has a certain deficit in terms of community. That deficit is partially compensated for, but in no sense attenuated, by the abstract solidarity which economic and social citizenship establishes and institutionalizes. The question of the relationship between society and community is raised in an illuminating way by Alain de Benoist when he writes:

> The dissolution of the old communities had been hastened by the birth of the nation-state, a *societal* phenomenon . . . which has been linked to the emergence of the individual . . . The communitarian problematic assumes renewed significance . . . when seen in terms of a return to small units of collective life developing apart from the great state and bureaucratic apparatuses which can no longer manage to play their traditional role today as integrative structures. Seen in this way, the community seems the natural framework for a local democracy – an organic, direct, grassroots democracy – based on more

active participation and on the re-creation of new local public spaces, as well as a means of resolving the major challenge thrown up by this century's end, namely: 'How is one successfully to achieve one's integration and assert one's identity without denying the diversity and specificity of its various components.' In pressing its claim as one of the possible forms for *transcending* modernity, the community loses the 'archaic' status sociology had long attributed to it.[4]

This could scarcely be put better, on condition that we specify that the community in question in this passage – a 'small unit of collective life', an 'organic, direct, grassroots democracy', a 'natural framework for a local democracy' – is of the kind Michael J. Sandel terms 'co-operative' and not the kind he, and Alain de Benoist following him, term 'constitutive'. What we are referring to here corresponds to the American-English term 'community', speaking of which Leo Löwenthal has pointed out that, in the United States, 'they think more in terms of small units, the neighbourhood unit, the place where you live, the community. The term "community", untranslatable into the continental European vocabulary, is of decisive importance in American life, as it refers to a field in which continuous actions are not just possible, but are demanded of everyone and actually carried out.'[5]

For its members, the co-operative community can be a source of strong allegiance and emotional security. However, it cannot provide a strong, changeless *identity*, as the constitutive community does. Because some communitarians (and, with them, Alain de Benoist) attempt to smuggle through the pre-eminence of the constitutive community in the baggage of the co-operative community, we shall make plain from the outset the distinction between these two forms.

The members of a constitutive community belong to that community by birth, irrespective of any deliberate commitment. They do so by having been imbued, as a result of their upbringing and, subsequently, their schooling, with (cultural, historical, spatial, etc.) references and customs common to all the inhabitants of their 'homeland'. The fact of belonging to the constitutive community *precedes any union between its members*. From the family community to the 'national community' (the *Volksgemeinschaft* or popular community, whether or not it is politically unified by a nation-state), with all the various stages of village, neighbourhood or street community in between, there are different gradations and levels of community membership. The more primal a place such membership occupies in the experience of individuals, shaping their understanding of themselves and of others, the greater is the strength of the community bond and the more immune it is from questioning: the kinship bond can be stretched, but it never breaks. It is the same with the village or neighbourhood one grew up in. The ties formed at school with children from one's neighbourhood can provide the basis for what may for ever remain the familiar world where one feels more 'at home' than anywhere else, bound together with the people with whom one shares this founding experience, this history, this common space. This is what Germans call *'Heimat'* and it is one of the dimensions which goes to make up what sociologists refer to as the 'life-world'.[6]

Because it is based on the experience and references shared by all its members, the constitutive community is homogeneous. Its members belong to it *equally*, whatever their position in society, their place on a scale of macro-social values, their moral choices or political persuasions. You belong to the Jewish or Chinese community, for example, simply by being Jewish or Chinese; you belong to your neighbourhood or village community (to your *Heimat*, your veterans' association, your former pupils' association) solely by dint of an experience and a history you share with your 'countrymen', your 'schoolfellows', your 'brothers-in-arms'. It is quite clear, however, that in a highly differentiated modern society the communal allegiances of each individual do not exhaust his/her reality, do not define *all that he/she is*.[7]

The fewer and more fragile the individuals' social ties, or the more problematic their place in society – if indeed they have one – the more their need for identity or dignity will seek recourse to an allegiance which situates them *outside the social field*. That non-social identity – whether it be biological, religious, territorial or ethnic – will be allotted the task of defining individuals in their totality; it will be asserted, against the claims of the environing society, as an integral identity excluding other determinations. It will be all that the individual is, all that the individual has to be.[8]

This is the root and meaning of all the so-called 'fundamentalisms' or 'integrisms'. They operate as substitute social identities, which protect individuals from social relations of competition and shelter their identities from the changing values, pressures and demands of the society around them. To define oneself biologically (by race or sex), ethnically (by one's original, ancestral roots) or religiously (by obedience to divine commandments) is a way of asserting the right to be as one is without having to defend or conquer one's rights in a shifting society where no one is definitively certain what he/she is and what he/she has to be, and where the political sphere is precisely the space allotted for conflict, change and the struggle for new rights.[9]

The idea of 'communitarian society' expresses nostalgia for a simple, transparent, pre-modern world in which society would operate like an originary community: each member's identity and rights would be grounded in his/her belonging to that community by birth. In such a society, that identity and those rights would depend not on what one *does*, but what one *is* – by birth. This kind of belonging and identity has inevitable racial connotations. We find this confirmed, whether we like it or not, in those ideologies in which membership of the 'national community' by birth is the source of everyone's determinate identity and rights, these latter being defined as *rights by birth, which are neither political, economic nor social* – and from which aliens are excluded. By elevating birth – that is to say, the origin of ancestors, the pure 'blood' of parents – into the basic criterion of each person's dignity and rights, the national-communitarian ideology makes it possible to conjure away differences of class, wealth and social position, and to repress conflicts between dominant and dominated as attacks on the unity and cohesion of the nation and the people.

This amounts to saying that national-communitarian ideology has a radically *anti-political* import: against the divisions and conflicts of modern society, it sets the unity of the community of origin. It ascribes the disintegration of that community to the baneful influence of alien elements (world Jewish conspiracy, international finance, cosmopolitan intellectuals, etc.), and it can conceive the restoration of unity only through the repression of all expressions of political conflict and social division or struggle: political, ethnic and cultural pluralism; freedom of speech and association; the right to strike. No identity other than membership of the nation by birth will be admitted.

Any conception which pretends to ground citizenship in nation-ality and which consequently confuses political rights with native rights runs the risk of veering off into national-communitarian total-itarianism. This is why Michael Walzer is prominent among com-munitarians in stressing the importance of distinguishing between society and community, citizenship and nationality. In an article that applies equally to Europe, he presents the United States as a 'politi-cal nation of cultural nationalities. Citizenship stands apart from any form of particularism: from the national, ethnic, racial and religious points of view, the State is neutral.' The nation is a 'nation of nationalities':

> All groups, precisely because they are scattered and intermingled, share a single political space, in which security, health, beauty and accessibility are collective values. Only citizens can defend these values – and only citizens who participate in politics in the broadest sense will know how to make that defence correctly . . . The more individual men and women stress their own particular identities, the more they must act resolutely as citizens. For that is the only way the nation of nationalities, the social association of social associations, will acquire cohesion in spite of the separation of individuals.[10]

The reader will have noticed that Walzer avoids the expres-sion 'community of communities'. Those originary communities which 'express themselves within civil society' – where they have created 'an extraordinary number of organizations devoted to reli-gious practices, social assistance, culture and mutual protection' – he terms 'nationalities'. But these communities, being absorbed in cul-tivating their differences, do not have a sufficient 'sense of the common good', a sense of citizenship.[11]

What is at issue here is nothing less than the 'constitutive' char-acter for the individual of the communal identity. If one takes the view, with Michael J. Sandel, whom Alain de Benoist follows on this point, that 'the community grounds the choices which the [individ-ual] makes'; if it is 'the values and practices which are expressed [in the community] which constitute [the individual] as a person'; and if, consequently, 'self-understanding amounts to discovering progres-sively what our identities and natures consist in', then 'the attach-ments and commitments constitutive' of personal identity are never – and can never be – matters of choice: 'The essential question is not "What am I to be?" "What type of life am I to lead?" but "Who am I?"[12]

Starting out from this 'essential question' will never lead to the 'sense of citizenship' understood as a good I have in common with other communities or with a wider community in which mine is embedded. The political question, the question of the political, will no longer be possible, even in the form in which Alain de Benoist poses it when he says:

> The right to difference is a principle and has value only as a generalization. In other words, I can only defend my difference legitimately as long as I recognize and respect the difference of others . . . As soon as you consider difference not as something which makes dialogue possible but as something which validates its rejection; when, consequently, you posit difference as an absolute, . . . you fall back into tribal nationalism.[13]

But it is just such 'tribal nationalism' which seems unfailingly 'normal' if, with Sandel, you take the view that any criticism or judgement is based on the specific values of my constitutive community's 'tradition' – values incommensurable with those of other cultural communities. Short of stipulating that 'recognition and respect' for the values of communities different from my own is itself a value common to the traditions of all communities and cultures – an argument far more universalist than the universalism communitarians commonly denounce in the writings of Habermas and Apel – Sandel's position (and that of de Benoist) leads quite simply to regarding it as legitimate *for each community to close off its own sovereign space and recognize that the others have the right – and even the duty – to do the same.* Communities would then co-exist alongside and external to one another, each defending its 'politically correct' position and each accepting that the others do the same in their own specific spaces. This equates, ultimately, with a politics of 'ethnic cleansing'.

Philosophically, Sandel's position amounts to an absolute relativism, in which all value-systems, traditions and traditional practices recognize each other as having equal dignity, and values and practices not rooted in a tradition are denied any legitimacy. The sexual mutilation of adolescent girls (female circumcision) will have to be considered legitimate, for example, because it forms part of a tradition, and the defence of the inviolability of the human person will necessarily be regarded as not so because it is incompatible with the stability of the traditional order. The principle guiding the relations between communities will not be dialogue, but the isolation of each in a stance of 'My community, right or wrong!' Dialogue will become possible, and recognition of the legitimacy of the existence of a plurality of constitutive identities will have 'the value of a general principle' and will guide the behaviour of all communities, only if those communities have a common political culture and a common public space. But such a space will need to be established, for it does not arise spontaneously out of each community's recognition of the other's specificity. By itself, such a recognition will lead more probably to a plurality of compartmentalized public spaces than to a single common one.

The practice of dialogue becomes possible in the end only if each community rises above the values constitutive of its identity, stands back from that identity and interprets it in relative terms as one identity among others – that is to say, understands it as 'difference'. Identity then no longer has the quasi-ontological status it has for Sandel. It is no longer 'our nature'. Between individuals constituted in their being by the values and practices of their respective communities – values and practices they are able neither to choose nor to question – it is not easy to see how dialogue might be possible, nor what there would be dialogue about.[14] *The general principle of the right to difference cannot be an intrinsic value of the constitutive communal identity.* That principle can only be *either* a legal obligation imposed from outside by the constitutionally established state on the communities existing in one and the same political space, within which the principle of secularity requires them to set aside their differences, *or* a limitation each community imposes on itself in the interests of all, in consideration of the *common space* in which they have to exist, which it is in their interest to treat as their common good.

In this latter case, the communities transcend the level of community and identity and move on to the political and societal plane, where values and practices are no longer determined on the basis of constitutive communal identity, but through political choices arrived at dialogically on the basis of principles, values and aims overriding communal identities and inducing each community to assume a reflexive distance from them. As Étienne Tassin writes, 'it is not from communal identity that a politically organized public space can arise, but from the political establishment of such a space that a common citizenship between peoples or communities can emerge.'[15]

However, the establishment of such a space is possible – that is to say, is accepted – only when it can be based on what Alain Touraine calls 'a democratic culture', into whose development it feeds back positively.[16] And democratic culture implies just this: that the members of the different communities do not claim their cultural identity to be a 'given' which constitutes them in their 'nature'; that they do not see it as something which can only be 'deepened', not questioned or subjected to choice. In fact, in the *'grandes sociétés'*, to use Serge Latouche's term once again, the community of origin cannot of itself be constitutive of 'who I am', since it is immersed in a much vaster context in which inherited values, practices and allegiances are not sufficient to orient and define me. The questions which arise for the citizen cannot be decided in terms of the inherited values, practices and traditions which constitute one's rooting in a stable 'life-world' immune from any possible challenge.

In a shifting and complex world, every constitutive community is forced to question the extent to which its traditional values continue to be valid. It is forced either to confirm those values or revise them, to question them or reflectively reaffirm them in the light of new situations. And it is the practical need to make these choices which will lead each community, immersed in a perpetually changing historical context, to differentiate itself or split into factions, as all religious communities, among others, have done, and to produce dissidents, rebels, oppositionists – in a word, *subjects* who claim the capacity to judge and choose for themselves. That is to say, who claim autonomy to be the ultimate and necessary foundation of values.

The political is the specific space in which to work out the conflictual tension between the opposing poles of community and society; or, to put it in Habermasian terms, the space to work out the tension between life-world and system, between the sphere of autonomy in which individuals and groups have a capacity for self-determination and self-regulation and the sphere of heteronomy, made up of constraints which arise from the operation of society as a set of institutions and apparatuses.

The capacity a society has to change, evolve and act on itself grows out of the tension between these two poles perpetually reacting back on each other. Everything which tends to efface the opposition between the two poles stifles political debate, conflict and thinking and propels society into an increasingly rigid, bureaucratic and authoritarian statism or into the stifling, strait-jacketed conformism of fundamentalist or national-communitarian societies.

Digression 2
Alain Touraine or
the Subject of Criticism

The problem of legitimate critique

The theoretical legitimacy and practical applicability of social criticism have remained major unresolved problems of critical theory. To be immune from moralistic idealism and ideological biases, critical theory aimed to be what Horkheimer in his early writings called 'the intellectual side of the historical process of emancipation'. In other words, the sociologist's critical approach would be justified only if it could uncover within the social reality forces, movements and practices embodying the theoretician's critical point of view. Theory had to reflect scientifically emancipatory actions in whose 'pre-scientific' reality its truth would be grounded.

This dialectical approach, quite obviously in keeping with historical materialism, demanded that the sociologist be able to detect what 'social forces' were asserting 'emancipatory interests' in their struggle against established forms of domination. The Frankfurt School originally considered the working class, in its struggle to assert the logic of 'living labour' against that of 'dead labour' (capital), to be the driving force of the 'historical process of emancipation'. But it could not identify any other social force after the working class had proved unable to resist National Socialism, Stalinism and the more subtle forms of social control exerted by the cultural manipulation of the consumer that were characteristic of affluent capitalism.

In its more extreme post-structuralist forms, social theory came to present society as a system dominated by mega-technological apparatuses, totally divorced from the life-world of social and cultural actors, perpetuating itself by instrumentalizing people's motives and vital energies in a way that would maximize its control over them. According to this view, a dehumanized system was producing dehumanized people who were nothing more than the tools of its self-reproducing power. Social critique could no longer find an anchorage in conflicts and actions that challenged the system.

A special mention must be reserved, however, for the most influential of the descendants of the Frankfurt School, Jürgen Habermas, who set out to show that social criticism can be revived by seeking its foundation not specifically in productive labour, but in the very essence of communicative social interactions. It is particularly instructive to compare Touraine's approach with that of Habermas, for both reject the theoretical positions of anti- or postmodernism, both understand modernity as originally emancipatory, both diagnose an increasing divorce between actors and system, subjective and objective meaning. But while converging on relevant political issues, there are basic theoretical differences between them.

Modernity: Habermas and Touraine

A wide area of agreement may be found between Habermas and Touraine in their efforts to reformulate Weber's conception of modernity and its crisis. Both think of modernity as a differentiation of the spheres of social action and life. These spheres become increasingly independent of each other, each generating its own logic, its own rational approach to the specific problems confronting it. The world grows increasingly complex and its complexity requires mechanisms of co-ordination and administration, which in turn require an increasing formalization of relations and procedures. For Touraine, the cultural world disintegrates into heterogeneous fragments:

> We have the impression of living in a fragmented world, in a non-society, because personality, culture, economics and politics all seem to be moving in different directions . . . And there appears to be no [unifying] principle to reunite [them] . . . The divorce between acts and meaning, between the economy and culture, provides the best definition of the crisis of modernity.[1]

Habermas points to the fact that there are two sides to this process. On the one hand, co-ordination of actions through 'steering media' (money, law, administrative regulations) 'eases the efforts and risks involved' in communicative interactions, renders the social world more predictable, reduces the dependence of individuals on the goodwill or good faith of others and emancipates them from the *personal* domination and power to which they are subjected in pre-modern societies. On the other hand, co-ordination through steering media reduces the spaces available for communicative co-operation and diminishes the need to seek reciprocal understanding. 'Social reality contracts into a reified organizational reality, which is inherently indifferent towards culture, society and personality . . . Formally organized spheres of action . . . solidify themselves into a kind of sociality devoid of norms.'[2]

The increasingly complex social system escapes intuitive comprehension, is divorced from communicative daily life practices and becomes accessible only to the 'counter-intuitive knowledge of the social sciences'. Thus morality and legality are divorced. Everyday culture is devalued and split into heterogeneous fragments. 'Culture, society and personality are divorced.' 'Subjective and objective meaning no longer coincide.' 'Social relations are split from the identity of actors.' This, according to Habermas, leads to the emergence of social 'movements of resistance' which 'aim to withdraw formally organized fields of action . . . from the power of steering media and to return these "liberated territories" to activities coordinated communicatively by the search for mutual understanding'.[3]

At first sight Touraine's diagnosis may seem strikingly similar. 'As a society becomes more modern,' he writes, 'it tends increasingly to be reduced . . . to a system of techniques and objects or to a technostructure.'[4] 'Nothing can prevent the world of production and power from drifting away from the world of individuals, their needs and their imaginary.'[5] 'There is no higher power and no arbitrating agency capable of affording effective protection to the essential interdependency of the two faces of modernity: . . . rationalization and subjectivation.'[6] For Touraine, therefore, 'society' can no longer be thought of as a 'totality'.

In underlining the similarities in Habermas's and Touraine's diagnoses, I have deliberately omitted semantic differences which point to their conflicting approaches. Habermas never refers to the social actor as a subject, whereas Touraine, as we shall see, believes that neither actor nor personal subject can exist without the other. The idea of the subject is replaced in Habermas's theory by that of the 'life-world', and it is in the name and from the viewpoint of the latter that social critique is legitimized, both theoretically and practically. Habermas is mainly concerned with the inroads which – as the complexity of the social environment and the autonomization of formalized spheres of action increase – co-ordinating steering media make into the life-world, that is, into the cultural resources enabling individuals to self-regulate their social interaction communicatively. According to Habermas, the rules of verbal exchange which make communicative action possible have a normative basis. They require that the understanding between individuals should be perfectly transparent and reciprocal, devoid of violence, cheating and relations of domination. Verbal communication implicitly refers to a norm of equality and perfect mutual comprehension, though empirically it may never live up to it.[7]

Life-world and subject: Touraine versus Habermas

Touraine presents several objections to this theory. 'Intersubjective communication,' he writes:

> is not a face-to-face confrontation of individuals; it is the encounter of social positions and of resources of power as much as of personal and collective imaginaries. Each individual is more constantly engaged in relations of dependence or co-operation than in verbal exchanges ... The individual is separated from him or herself by organizational and institutional situations containing numerous obstacles to the formation of an experience that could be exchanged with others ... Social, private and public relationships are clouded in an opacity which debate or argumentation will never dissipate.[8]

In other words, to live up to the ideal essence of verbal communication to which Habermas's *Diskursethik* refers, the participants would need to be personal subjects liberating themselves in their relationship from their social roles, hierarchical positions and unspoken certainties and prejudices. But the idea of such a subject-to-subject relation is totally unacceptable to Habermas, whereas it is central to Touraine's approach:

> The individual is not a subject by the will of God, but by its effort to disentangle itself from constraints and rules in order to self-organize

its experience . . . It is defined by its freedom, not by its roles . . . The individual may be called a subject . . . when he or she has fought those who invaded his/her personal life and imposed their orders.[9]

The differences in Habermas's and Touraine's approaches imply basic differences in their understanding of social conflict. In Habermas's view it is not the subject struggling for its self-determination, but the life-world, that builds up a resistance against the increasingly autonomized imperatives of formalized and technical subsystems. 'Systemic constraints . . . instrumentalize the life-world' (that is, use people's motives to make them realize unintended, alien goals in keeping with the system's requirements); they penetrate 'the pores of communicative action' and exert a 'structural violence entailing a systematic restriction of communication'.[10] The ensuing cultural impoverishment of the life-world and fragmentation of everyday relations 'robs consciousness of its synthesizing capacity', of its capability to give meaning, and leads to a breakdown of socialization. The 'symbolic reproduction of the life-world' is in jeopardy, and with it society itself, which at one point Habermas defines as 'the *systematically stabilized* interconnection of actions performed by *socially integrated* groups', or as a 'system fulfilling the conditions which will secure the maintenance of socio-cultural life-worlds'.[11]

But if the space for communicative action is restricted and its very possibility jeopardized by the destructive inroads of the logic of systems, how can communicative reason fight off the system's infringements upon a life-world which, according to Habermas, 'is its infrastructure'?[12] Does the crisis of the latter not necessarily entail the crisis of communicative co-operation and understanding? Is social critique, waged in the name and on the basis of communicative reason, not an *external* critique waged by a subject – the sociologist – positioning him/herself outside the society in which socio-cultural life-worlds are breaking down? Does not this critique therefore lose the very foundation on which its legitimacy and effectiveness were to be based, that is, its rootedness in social reality and practice?

As long as social criticism is made to depend on the integrity and vitality of the life-world as conceived by sociology, it stands in danger of remaining either abstractly theoretical or practically conservative. The very concept of the life-world as defined by Habermas and, before him, Schütz implies that its resistance or defence could not help being a resistance to change and innovation. For Schütz, the life-world is 'the everyday knowledge supplied by tradition, providing us with interpretations applicable to persons and events arising in our immediate environment';[13] while for Habermas it is the 'stock of self-evidences or unshakeable convictions used by participants for their co-operative communicative interpretation processes', the 'culturally transmitted stock of interpretation patterns', the 'unquestioning frame within which arise all problems that have to be mastered', 'the intuitive knowledge as to *how* to cope with a situation, *what* one can rely on in that situation'.[14]

As the system's increasing complexity transcends what the life-world can cope with, the latter becomes an increasingly 'provincial' subsystem; it loses its relevance, and so does communicative action, to the task of coping with reality. It is then to be expected that the life-world will resist the growing pressure of systemic constraints not by a rational critique of and action on the system, but by clinging defensively to the unquestioning intuitive self-evidences, and the customary, familiar, traditional ways of thinking, behaving, interacting and relating to the world. Its *irrelevance* to the novelty of situations will be seen to mean not that the elaboration of different approaches, certainties and modes of conduct is to be undertaken – for this would require the reflexivity and autonomy of the subject – but that the unfamiliar, complex, estranged reality is to be fought off as an inherently 'evil' attack on the 'true', 'natural', 'normal' order of things. It will not be the intuitive patterns of interpretation that are considered irrelevant, but a reality which exceeds their grasp. Their invalidation will be explained intuitively as a conspiracy of foreign powers – Jews, foreigners, rootless, cosmopolitan financiers – the betrayal of corrupt politicians and the negativism of hairsplitting intellectuals. The life-world will want to maintain its 'unquestionable certainties' by a passionate fundamentalist crusade against all that undermines it.

As long as their foundations are situated in the life-world as conceived by sociology, we must expect social criticism and cultural or political opposition to be conservative, traditionalist, parochial and anti-modern. This is an aspect of which Touraine – who has dealt extensively with the 'nostalgia for Being' – is quite aware, whereas it is hardly ever considered by the second-generation critical theorists. Axel Honneth's reinterpretation of Habermas, however, breaks some new and fertile ground for critical theory. Honneth gives central importance to Adorno's notion of 'the non-identical', that is, to activities and relations by which the subject differs from, resists or rejects functional identification with social roles or social usefulness.[15] For Honneth, the non-identical is not simply (as for Adorno) a residual category, but a dimension which, in modern or 'postmodern' societies, may be central to the individual's experience and lay the ground both for a critique of society and for opposition to the logic of instrumentality. The non-identical includes aesthetic experience as well as both public communicative relations and private ones, such as love, friendship or affection – none of which can be instrumentalized for ends other than its own.

Honneth thus shifts the emphasis away from the communicative reproduction of the life-world towards what he calls 'pathologies of social recognition'. These pathologies develop when individuals are denied social recognition for what they are, do, feel and want; in other words, when there is a conflict or contradiction between the reality of their experience and the patterns of social recognition and valuation. What they are expected to be is beyond them, and the things for which society is prepared to grant them recognition (their work, for instance) either are impossible for them for structural social reasons (for example, the organization of the labour market, structural unemployment, etc.) or clash with their own conception of what they deserve recognition for.

The individual set free

This is an important step forward in the direction of the idea of the subject, as set out in Touraine's *Critique of Modernity*. Indeed, the subject, as defined by Touraine, becomes the only possible foundation for legitimate and effective social critique, when the self-evidences, unquestionable convictions, social roles and identities are swept away by an ongoing process of social change and disintegration. Individuals can then no longer be explained and understood by their position in society, by what society expects from them or by what they are accustomed to expect from it. Functionalist sociological categories lose their relevance. Society is 'no more than a series of changes',[16] no more than a poorly integrated and badly controlled changing space in which techno-bureaucratic or commercial apparatuses of production, management and communication aim to reduce the individual to 'a mere consumer, a human resource or a target'.[17] 'All forms of functionalism, conservative or critical, are inapplicable to [these] situations in which the promotion of mobility is at least as important as the maintenance of order.'[18] Identification with a social or work role becomes impossible. Individuals are expected, on the contrary, to be prepared for continual changes: for changing jobs, skills, patterns of consumption, life-style, residence, etc. They are *set free* from social enrolment. The normative requirements of *social usefulness* no longer shape their lives and occupations. Indeed, society no longer has any use, any job, for an increasing proportion of its members. In one way or another, working and living are divorced, just as socially useful labour time is divorced from the time in which individuals produce themselves and seek to fill their lives with meaning and a sense of self-fulfilment.

Instrumental reason thus loses its grip on individual life. As the amount of labour required by the sphere of economic production and social reproduction shrinks, virtually unlimited spaces become available for the development of non-profit-making and non-instrumental activities – self-determined activities serving no formally predefined purpose: caring, communicative, self-help, educational and artistic activities, in both private and public spheres, self-organized networks of mutual assistance, non-monetarized exchange and self-producing. But all these activities must develop against the logic of the apparatuses of power. For as the growth of material production comes to a halt, as industrialism declines and as disposable time takes precedence over labour time in people's lives, economic, managerial and political power moves on to new ground. It no longer concentrates on dominating people solely as producers and consumers; it must now concentrate on dominating them in their disposable time as well, in the non-productive, non-material activities by which they produce *themselves*. It must prevent them from taking possession of the time liberated by labour-saving technologies and from using this time in ways by which they might regain their power over their personal and collective existence. To perpetuate itself, domination must commodify, professionalize, monetarize those activities – from bringing up children to house cleaning; from preparing meals and keeping oneself fit and clean to making love; from taking pleasure in doing things by oneself and for others to the enjoyment of leisure, etc. – in which the self-reliance of people and communities is rooted. The loosening of socialization and the potential increase in personal autonomy must then be depicted as a burden from which individuals are to be relieved by marketable substitute identities, made available by the fashion, communications, cultural, entertainment and health industries.

With the shift in the focus of domination and social control, what Touraine calls 'the central conflict' also moves on to new ground. The invasion of individuals' innermost capacities for self-determination foreshadows a dispossession that is even more total than the one they underwent as vendors of their labour power. For Touraine, the cultural critique of the consumer society now has something in common with the ethical and political critique of the totalitarian society. 'No individual, intellectual or not, living in the West at the end of the twentieth century, can escape the fear of a total loss of meaning, or the fear that private life and the capacity to be a Subject are being invaded by propaganda and advertising, by the degradation of society into a crowd, of love into pleasure.'[19] Resistance against this form of domination can come only from the subject defending its autonomy. This is what is at stake in the central conflict characteristic of the 'programmed society'.

Programmed society

The term 'programmed' is applied by Touraine to a society 'in which the production and mass distribution of cultural commodities play the central role that belonged to material commodities in the industrial society',[20] namely, the production and distribution of knowledge, medical care, information and self-images by the corresponding apparatuses. The working of these apparatuses implies that the thrust of rationalization needs to shift 'from the administration of things to the government of men'.[21] Managerial power now consists in 'predicting and modifying opinions, attitudes and modes of behaviour, and in moulding personalities and cultures'.[22] The conflict over the goals of cultural productions such as health, training, education and information is becoming an issue of greater importance than the conflict over who controls the means of material production. 'The object of conflicts in these areas is to defend a certain conception of freedom, and the ability to give a meaning to life':[23]

Should a hospital, in particular, be an organization ruled by a combination of professional, financial, administrative and corporate logics, or should it be patient-centred, so as to ensure that a patient is not simply an object of medical care, but also an informed subject with projects and a memory who has a voice in deciding what treatment he or she should receive and how it should be applied? This debate has not led to the emergence of organized actors or patients' unions. But it is present in everyone's mind and is often aired on television. The medical programmes which have the greatest impact are those which deal most directly with the theme of patients' responsibilities and rights in the context of euthanasia and palliative care, artificial insemination, or the treatment of serious illnesses.[24]

'The most vivid "contestations" of the establishment now have an ethical basis,' Touraine continues:

> for domination now affects bodies and souls rather than labour and juridical status . . . Individuals challenge the dominant logic of the system by asserting themselves to be subjects, by resisting the world of things and the objectification or commodification of their needs. This is why the idea of the subject cannot be divorced from an analysis which describes contemporary society as post-industrial or programmed rather than as post-modern . . . Public opinion, if not organized political life, is already giving expression to new conflicts and to the call for the complete transformation of a society whose cultural orientations are accepted by the social movements which are opposed to their social and political implementation.[25]

The central conflict redefined

In previous writings Touraine defined the 'central conflict' as a conflict between 'the dominated and the dominating' over 'the use society will make of its own capacity to act upon itself', this capacity being 'the central stake at issue'. 'Classes fight for the . . . management of the means whereby society produces itself . . . The dominated class . . . fights for a collective reappropriation' of these means.[26] In Touraine's more recent writings these definitions have been slightly shifted and radicalized, since the 'means' whose application is at issue in the central conflict ubiquitously pervade all the social as well as private spheres of life. The dominated and the dominating can no longer be described as identifiable classes. The central conflict has no central front any more; its front may be said to be everywhere, and its actors can no longer be classified according to traditional sociological or even social categories. The meaning of these conflicts and the stakes at issue become intelligible only from the standpoint of the subject 'as central principle', rejecting 'the self-image society forces upon it'. Conversely, the existence of the subject 'becomes intelligible only through the hermeneutic search for the inseparable unity and diversity of all the rifts in the established order, of all the calls for freedom and responsibility.'[27] This is the end of sociological objectivism or scientism, since the subject cannot be investigated, deduced and identified with methods of empirical positivistic sociology. It is, as Touraine points out, 'a non-social principle', a self-founding and self-creating point of departure, not of arrival. It can be apprehended, discovered, understood in its self-assertions only by sociologists who themselves are, and understand themselves to be, self-asserting subjects.

The sociologist must consequently place him/herself inside the subject-actors' movements as a participating analyst and:

> consider them not as objects to be studied, but as bearers of the meaning of their action, which is to be made as self-conscious as possible by freeing it from the pressures of ideology and politics . . . The researchers . . . , without identifying with the group, make themselves the representatives of the highest possible meaning of its action. If the group, siding with the analysis, makes their hypotheses its own, because they increase the intelligibility of what it is undertaking, then the pertinence of those hypotheses is confirmed.[28]

Touraine's theoretical approach and practical method are based on two implicit prerequisites which deserve closer examination. First, the social movements to which Touraine's method is applicable must call for fundamental transformations of society. These transformations are to be sought by actions *from within* this society and its cultural orientations, by using 'its capacity to act upon itself' against the interests and logic of the forces of domination. This requires that society be 'open' to transformation and not totalitarian or dictatorial. It also requires that the 'means by which society acts upon itself' be of a sort which allows them to be used for conflicting purposes or, as Touraine sometimes puts it, speaking of technology, that they be 'neutral'. Though they may be used currently for purposes of domination, they may also serve alternative purposes and break the dominating powers' hold upon society.

The 'neutrality' or ambivalence of the means by which modern societies act upon themselves should not be construed to mean, however, that they can all serve purposes of liberation or of domination *equally*. Some technologies, for example (this is a point on which Touraine sometimes lacks clarity), are structurally biased in favour of an enhanced domination of capital over labour and of commercial interests over those of the consumer. For this reason, opening up technological choices to public debate and evaluation is one of the most important concerns of the potentially radical social movements, uniting trade-union militants, environmentalists and consumer associations.

But the point Touraine seeks to make is a more fundamental one. Modern societies, he insists repeatedly, are neither social *orders* nor closed systemic *totalities*. Being riven by conflicts between a plurality of values, rationalities and purposes, they are structurally capable of evolution and change brought about by actions from *within*. They are not totalitarian systems needing to be overthrown and destroyed outright; and those fundamentalist groups – whether religious, 'deep ecologist', racist, ethnic or Marxist-Leninist-Maoist – who fight modern society from without as being inherently evil are fighting not a total system in the name of freedom, but an imperfect modernity and freedom in the name of a totally integrated, social-natural order. On this matter Touraine is an avowed reformist, considering revolution to be a pre-modern concept leading to totalitarian regimes.

Second, the social movements to which Touraine's approach is applicable must have an (at least potentially) emancipatory meaning. Their actors must understand themselves, or at least be potentially willing to understand themselves, as subjects fighting for their autonomy. For only subjects understanding themselves as such will consent reflectively to examine their motives and the meaning of their action. It will be extremely difficult, even downright impossible, to extend Touraine's method of investigation to movements or groups whose members are driven by that passion to *be* (that is to say, *not to exist* as subjects) and to 'escape from freedom' – as Erich Fromm puts it in his remarkable analysis of National Socialist ideology[29] – by claiming to be the tools of some superhuman will, calling, necessity, truth or essence which, by its very definition, cannot and must not be questioned, analysed, interpreted. From the point of view of the subject, the ideology of such movements and groups is based on the subject's ability *to deny its own existence, including this self-denegation itself* (this, by the way, is Sartre's definition of 'bad faith'),[30] by shutting itself off behind a totally organized, impenetrable system of arguments, dogmas and sacred truths, any attack on which must be repelled as a sacrilegious crime. Fanatics and dogmatists refuse to be understood by anyone – they want to be respected and feared – since whoever seeks to understand them credits them with an existence as subjects, which is precisely what they reject. When the skilful approach of social workers succeeds in involving individual fanatics in a conversation which, by making them feel understood, makes them aware of themselves as 'bearers of the meanings of their action', their 'faith' will tend to become unsustainable. We find once again here that Habermas's 'communicative reason' involves the autonomy and self-reflective capacity of Touraine's subjects.

In Touraine's approach, social critique and the subject's capacity for self-understanding are inseparably bound up with each other. The source and foundation of social critique is the subject itself, and the sociologist's task is to raise the subject's reflective self-understanding to the highest possible level. Self-evidence is no longer – as it was with the life-world – rooted in and legitimized by tradition and unquestioned inherited certainties. It is now rooted in the subject-actors' self-understanding of the meaning and reality of what they are fighting against and for. This, in my opinion, is the only convincing solution to the dilemma of critical theory. In Touraine, the subject of emancipation and the subject of theory tend to be reconciled and to recognize each other as two complementary sides of one and the same practice. This will lead Touraine to reject and subvert traditional sociology and its effort to explain the individual as the product of a society which is considered to be the 'true' or 'ultimate' subject. The passages from *Critique of Modernity* which I shall examine in the following section are quite enlightening in this regard.

Sociology subverted

For Touraine, 'the central history of modernity is that of the transition from the subject's struggles against the sacred order – in which the subject and rationalism were allies – to the subject's struggle against rationalizing models.'[31] Because 'rationalization tends to be closely bound up with the action of the ruling forces', that is, of industrial and state power, 'the defence of the subject immediately comes into conflict with the positivism and the technocracy of modern society and its management and control apparatuses.'[32] 'The subject is always a *bad subject* who rebels against rules and integration in an attempt to assert itself and enjoy [being] itself, and it is by resisting power' – by resisting apparatuses or *'the total apparatus known as society'* – (italics mine, A.G.) – 'that self-assertion is transformed into the will to be a subject'.[33] 'The subject can . . . manifest itself and act only by struggling for its liberation and by expanding the internal space in which desire and the law are not contradictory. The subject is constituted in the struggle against the anti-subject', against 'the logics of apparatuses and power.'[34] 'The subject can be defined only as an actor involved in social conflicts.'[35] Touraine's insistence on the conflictual character of actions which both reveal the emergence of the subject and produce it reflexively is directed implicitly against, on the one hand, functionalist or systematist social theory and, on the other, privatistic or individualistic interpretations which portray the subject as reflexively concerned with its own self-image, as 'obsessed with his or her identity', as Touraine puts it.

'Sociology', remarks Touraine:

> came into being by defining the good in terms of the social utility of the modes of behaviour it observed . . . The good was the contribution made by an actor – or, more accurately, an organ – to the workings of the social body . . . Individuals [were] therefore defined by their status and by their corresponding roles, or in other words the behaviour expected of them by others. [They were expected to fulfil their role] in accordance with models inscribed . . . in contemporary mores and ideas.[36]

Considering functionality to be the criterion of good, functionalist social theory had a markedly conservative and elitist bias. It could not pay attention to the 'non-rational beings – women, children, workers and the colonized – whose rebellion provides the starting-point for our discussion'.[37] 'The kind of sociology this book is attacking takes social usefulness . . . as a criterion of morality and refers to forms of behaviour that upset the order of things as marginal or deviant.' Claiming to be 'more positive or empirical' because it ignores the subject ('the I'), it is:

> actively supporting the forces of socio-cultural and ideological control which give the system its continued stranglehold on actors. These

forces replace the subject with the individual consumer of commodities and norms, and historicity with the reproduction of established values, norms and forms of organization. The reference to the subject is . . . a central principle that allows us to analyse all manifestations of individual and collective life.[38]

It alone enables 'many of the best sociologists' to perceive 'the breakdown of the correspondence between system and actors', between institutions and individuals, and to see that 'what is known as social integration can be reinterpreted as the controls exerted by power centres over social actors who are being increasingly manipulated' and who reassert themselves as subjects by protecting their freedom 'against an over-organized society'.[39]

In a complete reversal of perspectives, 'the good is now defined in terms of respect for the subject . . . Evil is the power which reduces the subject to the status of a human resource for the production of wealth, might or information', thus reducing 'other people's capacity for autonomous action'.[40] 'If sociology does not take the side of the subject against society, it is fated to be an ideological instrument promoting social integration and socialization.'[41]

Subject versus self

Touraine places great emphasis on the sharp contrast between the idea of the subject and that of the self. 'The normalization and objectification of human beings produce the Self,' he writes, 'whereas the I is constituted through resistance to power centres which are perceived as repressive.'[42]

In much the same way as Sartre,[43] Touraine sees the self and the ego as psychic objects, constructed by a self-denying subject in its effort to be for itself the other which it wants to be for the others. Ego and self, remarks Touraine, are constructed 'from the outside by social roles'.[44] The self is 'defined only by the expectations of others and controlled by institutional rules'.[45] By contrast, the subject exists as such only when it recognizes 'the non-correspondence between social roles, the self-images lent to me or forced upon me by society, and my assertion of myself as a subject creating my existence'.[46] It is not 'the moralizing discourses of those who speak of nothing but social integration', but 'our non-belonging . . . [our] ability to stand aside from our own social roles . . . and our need to protest that allows each of us to live as a subject . . . Subjectivation is always the antithesis of socialization . . . *provided that we do not become trapped into a counter-culture of subjectivity . . . and commit ourselves to the struggle against the forces that actively destroy the subject'.*[47]

This is a far cry from the preoccupation with self-identity. Touraine's idea of the subject is akin to Honneth's understanding of the 'non-identical'. Love and friendship are shown by Touraine to be experiences crucial to the subject's emergence, since they involve a commitment to another subject 'beyond the limits of what is permitted or forbidden', a commitment 'too absolute to be social', leading to the rejection of 'all social or personal bonds', and even of 'patterns of consumption and adaptation'. Love and eroticism are without any social functionality, 'doing away with social determinisms and giving the individual the desire to be an actor, to invent a situation rather than to conform to one'.[48] Hence their central importance for modernity.

In contrast to Giddens's self-preoccupied individual, whose activities aim less at changing or inventing a situation than at reflexively sustaining a self-identity matching 'the ideal self', that is, 'the self I want to be',[49] Touraine's subject is 'a dissident, a resistance fighter',[50] shaping itself at the antipodes of the care for the self by defending freedom against power, transforming him/herself into an actor able to transform a situation. Because, as Sartre would have said, its project is not one of *being* (as implied in the idea of identity), but an appeal to freedom challenging the logic of systems, the subject is this 'least social element in human individuals'[51] upon which our resistance to social power must be based, especially in the consumer society. Unless 'self-identity' is understood, inappositely, as a synonym of 'self-determination', the preoccupation with self-identity is likely, on the contrary, to play into the hands of culture industries thriving on the supply of differentiated models, patterns and elements for the self-construction of individual identities. 'It is the organization [of society] that constructs needs which, whilst they are certainly not artificial, do conform to the interests of power.'[52] Power centres do as much to create consumers, voters and a public as they do to respond to social demands. If they do not construct themselves as subjects, individuals will have their behaviour determined by decision-making centres that can predict what people will like, demand and purchase, including their self-images. The consumer him/herself is a commodity produced by marketing or 'communications' industries, sold to and bought by producers seeking to retain or enlarge their share of the market. Demand is engineered, consumption is socially redefined, the self-image of the consumer is sold to him/her as intrinsic to the commodity's use-value. 'Ascribed status' has never been more important than in this society, notes Touraine, nor has the hold of decision-making centres over the lived experience of individuals and groups. The public field now includes preoccupations which extend far beyond social and political realities.[53]

True, in the disintegrating modern society, the individual 'has no choice but to choose', as Giddens, using a Sartrean formula, remarks.[54] But this choice may well be a trivially mundane rather than a genuinely autonomous one – a choice between different brands or prefabricated self-images – unless the subject chooses the autonomy into which it is thrown, discovers, behind the dominant ideology of 'free choice', relations of power and dependence, aggressiveness and scarcity, and rejects the self-images, roles and identities supplied by the system as irrelevant to its aspirations and desires.

This is precisely the kind of self-assertion of the subject portrayed in *Nicht so wie unsere Eltern*, Rainer Zoll's investigation into changed attitudes to work and social roles.[55] Speaking of the 'unprecedented variety and wealth of opportunities from which to choose', young people declare that none of the choices open to them has 'enough consistency and meaning to warrant a commitment. None could justify a person's identification with it.' What sociology often describes as a search and need for identity shows itself here as a perpetually frustrated search and need for meaning, identity being rather a surrogate for the latter. For only a subject can create meaning. Communities or strongly integrated, mobilized and hierarchized social orders, however, can supply identities to their members and spare them the trouble of searching for a meaning by themselves.

Exit society

The issue in hyper-modern societies, therefore, is not so much the lack of opportunities for acquiring an identity in conformity with 'the Self I want to be' as the lack of opportunities for meaningful *activities* through which individuals could produce both liberated social relations based on mutual recognition, and themselves as sub-

jects of their *action*. For *when you cannot define yourself by what you
do, all that is left is what you are*. As Touraine puts it, 'anyone who is
no longer defined by their activity soon constructs or reconstructs
an identity based upon their origins.'[56] What Giddens appropriately
calls the 'disembedding of social relations by abstract systems'[57] gives
birth to 'a system without actors' and to powerless 'actors without
a system, trapped into their imagination and their memories'.[58]
Seeking refuge in the protective shell of their cultural-ethnic
oneness, they reject the modernity they can see only from the
outside, as a present holding no future for them. Culturalism, racism,
fundamentalism are the resentfully aggressive defences by which the
victims of apparatuses of power governed by the abstract logic of
markets, money and profit attempt to preserve a sense of together-
ness and self-esteem. The price they have to pay, though, is high:
total loyalty and submission to the community's traditions, rites and
leaders; total self-denegation by the individual of his/her freedom.

    This leads Touraine to insist on the necessary complementarity of
the freedom-subject and the community-subject, of rationalization
and cultural identity. The subject as freedom is inseparable from both
the rationalization that protects from a 'suffocating socialization',[59]
and the cultural roots which preserve it from being reduced to a
manipulated consumer or a rational producer. The 'two faces of the
subject'[60] must always be present together if it is to resist both modes
of its destruction by the order of technology or the order of religion.
'Critical reason'[61] protects personal freedom against communitarian
immobility. But combining these two dimensions of the subject's
existence does not mean that they can be *reconciled*, let alone unified.
The values of rationality and of cultural specificity are conflicting
and their conflict cannot be abolished, only mediated. The tension
between them – the tensions between community and system,
between the subject as a 'being of desire' and the subject as rationalizing agent – are essential to modernity. They generate a 'void at
the centre of society', a void that must be preserved since it is the
space where political debates, deliberation and choices can take place
regarding the best way to balance the relative importance of modernity's two dimensions.[62]

    'Modernity rejects the idea of society,' Touraine continues, 'and
replaces it with that of social change.' Social life is 'a set of relations
between the social actors of change'.[63] There can be no democracy
without the subject's willingness and ability to take advantage of this

tension and to roll back both the power of apparatuses and the 'obsession with identity',[64] to enlarge the space where it can experience itself as a creatively free combination of 'the shattered fragments of modernity',[65] knitting between them (between Eros, the nation, consumption and production) 'a network of complementary and antagonistic relations'[66] and refusing to identify with any one of them. 'The democratic order must be redefined as a combination, ruled by no superior principle, of the internal logics of particular social (sub-)systems and the self-proclaimed autonomy of the subject.' 'The separation of actor and system, citizen and State, appears to be the only response to . . . the totalitarian threats on one side, the rule of a neo-corporatist or hyper-liberal market, on the other.'[67]

I know of no emerging social movement which matches these definitions more completely than the nebula of groups, circles of trade-union militants, local politicians, left intellectuals, social workers, economists, religious associations, associations of old-age pensioners and the jobless, all of which want to see beyond the disintegration of the 'work-based' (more accurately: 'job-based') society and fight for an alternative implying less market, less state, more self-organized civil society, based on a different use of one of the most important 'means by which society acts upon itself'. I am referring to the multi-faceted movement for an alternative use and distribution of a key resource – disposable time – generated by labour-saving technologies. The significance of this movement resides in the way in which it combines rationalization with subjectivation in its aims.

In the name of the subject as reason, it rejects the irrational capitalist management of technological rationalization, as a result of which increasing gains in productivity generate falling wages, deteriorating living and working conditions, a rapidly growing underclass of working poor, destitute, jobless and homeless people on one side, and rising profits, affluence and conspicuous luxuries on the other. Instead of liberating people from poverty, toil, stress and stupefying work, labour-saving technologies are used to strengthen the domination which capital, via the logic of markets, exerts on all aspects of people's working and living conditions. Rejecting also the anti-modernist demand of conservative politicians who want to reduce productivity so that a greater number of workers may be employed at very low wages to accomplish a given task, the movement demands that both socially produced wealth and socially required labour should be redistributed in such a way as to enable everyone to work less and less for an adequate and secure income.

This rationalization is explicitly demanded in the name of the subject as freedom. Its purpose is 'to roll back the might of apparatuses', the domination of the logic of capital, power, technology and administration. The movement promotes practices, concepts and values outlining an alternative to the job-based consumer society; that of a society of 'full activity', not 'full employment'; where the disposable time made available by the reduction of the number of hours worked per week, month, year or decade could lead to the development of self-organizing networks of voluntary co-operation, mutual help and self-producing, and to a corresponding self-definition of needs and self-restraint in the consumption of commodities; where the balance between giving and sharing on the one hand, selling and buying on the other, between self-producing and waged work, between free self-activity and occupations functional to the requirements of apparatuses, would be shifted in favour of the subject's individual and collective liberation from the logic of markets and systems; where everyone would lead several lives – as a job holder, a citizen, a private person, a member of a community, association or neighbourhood – and would combine them with the 'never-ending but happy task of constructing a life as though it were a work of art constructed out of disparate raw materials'.[68]

The society which doled out identities, positions and allegiances no longer exists. As Jean-Marie Vincent puts it:

> We have to give up the idea of perfectly harmonious relations between individuals, groups and society . . . Society is nothing but a constellation of groups, networks of interaction and shifting norms. Only by dint of the dominance of practico-technical apparatuses of valorization or State power does it seem unified. What we have to pursue, therefore, is a variable, differential sociality produced by a profusion of communications and perpetually self-renewing sequences of activity, enabling individuals really to accumulate experience, broaden their horizons and transform themselves permanently.[69]

The main concern of sociologists must be to determine the meaning of 'the cultural fields and conflicts, and the forms of political action that are being reorganized before our eyes':[70]

To discover the meaning of not only new ideas, but practices of all kinds, individual and collective, which reveal the issues, actors and conflicts of a new world. Our world is dominated by strategies for making profits or gaining power, but it is also alive with liberating utopias, communitarian defences, erotic images, humanitarian campaigns, attempts to catch the eye of the other. These are the scattered fragments that will together construct a Subject which can reconcile reason and freedom, intimacy and community, commitment and non-commitment.[71]

Notes

Introduction

1 Jeremy Rifkin, *The End of Work*, G. P. Putnam & Sons, New York, 1995.

2 Perret is the author of *L'Avenir du travail: les démocraties face au chômage*, Le Seuil, Paris, 1995. He is a supporter of the idea of transitional labour markets proposed by Günther Schmid. He argues that jobs (in the sense of paid work) are becoming increasingly personal and that there is 'an increasing substitutability between professional activities and non-professional passions' (ibid., p. 180). [Trans.]

3 On this subject, see the very concrete and illuminating article by Bo Rothstein, 'Critique de l'État-providence', in J.-P. Durand (ed.), *La Fin du modèle suédois*, Syros, Paris, 1994.

4 Better than any other writer, Jacques Robin has brought out the multiple dimensions of this mutation, which 'affects not only our conceptual vision of the world but our means of apprehending reality'. He shows that it introduces a 'fundamental break' into the history of humanity: it puts an end to the 'energy era' which, since the beginning of the Neolithic, has striven to transform matter by harnessing ever more powerful sources of energy. The information revolution throws capitalist economy and society and, more fundamentally, capitalist civilization into crisis. See J. Robin, *Changer d'ère*, Le Seuil, Paris, 1989, especially chs 1 and 5. Cf. Robin, *Quand le travail quitte la société industrielle*, 2 vols, Groupe de réflexion inter- et transdisciplinaire (GRIT), Paris (21, boulevard de Grenelle), 1993–4.

5 Lester Thurow, *The Future of Capitalism*, William Morrow, New York, 1995, p. 309.

6 Rifkin, *The End of Work*, p. 177; Robert Reich, *The Work of Nations: Preparing Ourselves for 21st Century Capitalism*, Random House, New York, 1992, pp. 302–3.

7 Thurow, *The Future of Capitalism*, pp. 256–8.

8 See André Gorz, *Strategy for Labour*, Beacon Press, Boston, 1967, and *Socialism and Revolution*, Anchor Books/Doubleday, New York, 1973, and Allen Lane/Penguin Books, London, 1975, ch. 4.

9 Henri Maler, *Convoiter l'impossible. L'Utopie avec Marx, malgré Marx*, Albin Michel, Paris, 1995.

10 Jacques Bidet, 'Il n'y a pas de communisme après le socialisme', a paper delivered to the Institut de recherches marxistes, 15 May 1993. Jacques Bidet is co-director, with Jacques Texier, of the journal *Actuel Marx*, published by Presses Universitaires de France (PUF), and the author of, among other works, *Théorie de la modernité*, PUF, Paris, 1990.

Chapter 1 From the Social State to the Capital State

1 Q. Hoare and G. Nowell-Smith (eds), *Selections from the Prison Notebooks of Antonio Gramsci*, Lawrence and Wishart, London, 1971, p. 160.

2 Lester Thurow, *The Future of Capitalism*, William Morrow, New York, 1995, p. 180.

3 For a sense of the joyously subversive radicalism of the movements of this period, see (or look again at) Alexis Chassagne and Gaston Montracher, *La Fin du travail*, Stock 2, Paris, 1978. This is a compilation of extracts from French, American and Italian books and periodicals, from Situationist, anarchist or Marxist texts, in which 'Down with work!' is a recurring refrain. See also Bifo [Franco Berardi], *Le Ciel est enfin tombé sur la Terre*, Le Seuil, Paris, 1978.

4 P. Ingrao and R. Rossanda (eds), *Appuntamenti di fine secolo*, Manifesto libri, Rome, 1995. The second half of this quotation provides an excellent definition of what Adorno called the category of the 'non-Subject of Criticism'.

5 Marco Revelli, 'Economia e modello sociale nel passagio tra fordismo e toyotismo', in Ingrao and Rossanda (eds), *Appuntamenti di fine secolo*, pp. 211–13.

6 P.-N. Giraud, *L'Inégalité du monde*, Gallimard, Paris, 1996, pp. 222–3. My emphasis.

7 The figures are Jeremy Rifkin's. See Rifkin, *The End of Work*, G. P. Putnam & Sons, New York, 1995, pp. 166–73.

8 James Petras and Todd Cavaluzzi, 'Devenir pauvre en travaillant', *Le Monde diplomatique*, 508, July 1996, p. 11.

9 Alain Lipietz, *La Société en sablier*, La Découverte, Paris, 1996.

10 See especially Norbert Reuter, 'Export als Droge', *Die Zeit*, 8 November 1996.

11 See François Chesnais, *La Mondialisation du capital*, Syros, Paris, 1995.

12 UNCTAD Report, 1994, and Chesnais, *La Mondialisation du capital*.

13 Quoted by Lipietz, *La Société en sablier*, p. 313.

14 Giraud, *L'Inégalité du monde*, p. 224.

15 Ibid., pp. 277–8.

16 Ibid.

17 The so-called management centres enable any company to avoid taxes on profits or gains altogether. The centre itself pays only a small, fixed amount of tax.

18 On this, see René Passet, 'La grande mystification des fonds de pension', *Le Monde diplomatique*, 516, March 1997.

19 See James Tobin, 'A Proposal for International Monetary Reform', *Eastern Economic Journal*, 3–4, July–October 1978.

20 J. Eichgreen, J. Tobin and C. Wyplosz, 'Two Cases for Sand in the Wheels of International Finance', *Economic Journal*, 105, 1995. In *Die Globalisierungsfalle*, Rowohlt, Hamburg, 1996, pp. 118–23, H.-P. Martin and H. Schumann give a very good summary of the objections and debates sparked off by Tobin's proposal in politico-financial circles.

21 Lipietz, *La Société en sablier*, pp. 318–22.

22 In Thurow's view (*The Future of Capitalism*, p. 136), only the European Union would have the means to impose other rules for international trade, including rules for relations with peripheral countries. For a similar argument, see Martin and Schumann, *Die Globalisierungsfalle*, pp. 299–307, 322–3.

23 P. Viveret, 'Monnaie et citoyenneté européenne', *Transversales*, 42, November–December 1996. This article convincingly develops the argument suggested by ex-Chancellor Helmut Schmidt in *Le Monde* of 9 November 1996. In constantly hardening the convergence criteria laid down in the Maastricht Treaty, the Bundesbank is attempting to sink the Euro by turning the peoples of Europe (including the Germans) against the single currency, which is coming, as a result of their actions, to have exorbitant social costs. Even if the Euro is introduced as planned, the monetarist, anti-social and structurally deflationary policy that one would expect would be imposed on Europe through economic rule by a sovereign central bank will sooner or later bring about the disintegration of the EU. In short, the strategy of global finance capital consists in using the Euro to sink the Euro and the European Union to sink the European Union. And this would all be done in the interests of the hegemony of the dollar, seconded by the Deutschmark, when it was, in actual fact, the original aim of the single currency to end that hegemony.

24 Lipietz, *La Société en sablier*, p. 326; Giraud concretely demonstrates the mutually advantageous character of such a policy in *L'Inégalité du monde*, pp. 314–15.

25 In a famous article published by *The Economist Asia Survey* of 30 October 1993, Jim Rohwer predicted that by the year 2000 Asia would have 400 million consumers with purchasing power 'at least equal to the rich-world average today . . . The zooming growth and absolute size of Asia's middle class should therefore create some of the biggest business and financial opportunities in history, and far-sighted Western firms and their workers stand to profit immensely from this.' Quoted by Richard Smith, 'China and the Global Environment', *New Left Review*, 222, March–April 1997. For a population of almost 950 million, at the beginning of the 1990s India had only 600,000 households with an annual income of 10,000 dollars or more.

26 R. Machetzki, 'Kein Kampf der Kulturen', *Die Zeit*, 10, 1 March 1996, p. 14. The author is a researcher at the Institute for Asian Studies (Institut für Asienkunde), Hamburg. The reference within the article is to George Hicks, 'The Myth of the Asian Century', *Asian Wall Street Journal*, 26 October 1995.

27 Machetzki, ibid.

28 Kenichi Ohmae, *The End of the Nation State: The Rise of Regional Economies*, HarperCollins, London, 1996, pp. 101–15. Ohmae is a former senior partner of the consultants McKinsey and Co.

29 Paul Virilio, 'De la géopolitique à la métropolitique', *Transversales*, 41. The text in question is an extract from *La Ville et la guerre*, Éditions de l'imprimeur, Ministère de la Défense, Paris, 1996.

30 The International Labour Office (ILO) defines as unemployed those persons who cannot provide for themselves from their work.

31 See Smith, 'China and the Global Environment'.

32 Jacques Robin, 'Occidentalisation et mondialisation: le prix à payer', *Savoirs/Le Monde diplomatique*, 2 ('Une terre en renaissance. Les semences du développement durable'), 1993, p. 53.

33 According to the World Bank's 1995 Report, the world's working population will rise from a current figure of 2,500 million to 3,700 million by 2025. The current world unemployment rate is already above 25 per cent, if in fact such a concept has any meaning.

34 I. Sachs, 'L'urbanisation ou la déruralisation?', *Transversales*, 41, September–October 1996.

35 See J. Rifkin, 'Automating the Third World', in *The End of Work*, pp. 203–7.

36 Viewed in terms of income per head, the Catholic and Communist state of Kerala on the south-west coast of India is one of the poorest of the Indian Federation. However, its 'human development indicator' (HDI), the measure by which the United Nations Development Programme gauges the quality of life of peoples, is much higher than that of the richest states.

37 A. Toffler, *The Third Wave*, William Collins Sons, London, 1980. One should in particular read, or re-read, in this monumental work, which was rejected with stupidly sectarian contempt by Marxists, ch. 23, entitled 'Ghandi with Satellites'. This radical critique of what Serge Latouche was to call 'the Westernization of the world' shows the possibility of integrating third-wave technologies (micro-electronics) with the culture of pre-industrial societies. See also ch. 20, 'The Rise of the Prosumer', in which Toffler shows that 'what appears to be inefficient in conventional . . . [market] terms is, in fact, tremendously efficient when we look at the whole economy and not just part of it', p. 299.

Chapter 2 The Latest Forms of Work

1 The method of 'Motion and Time Measuring' logged to one-hundredth of a second each of the movements involved in assembly-line operations. Each of these took between 50 seconds and 3 minutes.

2 William Foote Whyte, *Money and Motivation. An Analysis of Incentive in Industry*, Harper and Row, New York, 1955, pp. 65–6.

3 See W. Womack (ed.), *The Machine that Changed the World*, HarperCollins, New York, 1990.

4 The factory in question is the New United Motor and Manufacturing Inc. (NUMMI). Ikebuchi's remarks are reported by J. Krafcik of MIT. See *Technology Review*, January 1992.

5 Quoted by Benjamin Coriat, *Penser à l'envers*, Christian Bourgois, Paris, 1991, p. 20.

6 As Benjamin Coriat shows, in his analysis of Ohno's writings in particular, '*kan-ban*' consists essentially in 'thinking' the manufacturing process 'from front to back'. Instead of first bringing together enormous stocks of parts and materials in the stores of a large factory, on which the assembly shops will draw, the *kan-ban* principle is to start out from orders for finished products which come to the final assembly plant and to 'back' order the parts and materials the teams of workers need to put together a particular model of the product that has just been ordered. In this way, 'there is in production . . . only the exact quantity of parts needed to satisfy the order [for the finished product]. This is how the "zero stock" principle which characterizes *kan-ban* is implemented.' B. Coriat, *L'Atelier et le robot*, Christian Bourgois, Paris, 1990, pp. 90–1.

Orders have to be passed back up the chain of production extremely quickly and reliably, and parts have to be produced and made available just as quickly. The whole of production is done on a 'just-in-time' basis. In many cases, less than one hour elapses between a part being ordered and entering the production process.

7 The expression 'general intellect' has become the rallying cry of an important school of Marxist thought. And this in spite of the fact that the expression was only used by Marx on one occasion, imprecisely and in passing, in the stunning ten pages or so of the *Grundrisse* which deal with automation, the hegemony of non-material work which ensues from it and the impossibility of taking labour time as the measure of labour any longer, or labour as the measure of wealth produced. The passage in question says: 'The development of fixed capital indicates to what degree general social knowledge has become a direct force of production, and to what degree, hence, the conditions of the process of social life itself have come under the control of the general intellect.' Karl Marx, *Grundrisse*, Penguin Books, Harmondsworth, 1973, p. 706; the terms 'general intellect' and 'knowledge' are in English in the original.

8 Japanese official surveys show that between two-thirds and three-quarters of final assembly workers in the car industry complain of chronic fatigue and exhaustion at the end of the working day. The big companies move these workers to less strenuous posts at the age of 30. Instances of people dying from overwork (*karoshi*) are not exceptional.

9 A public discussion between the national secretary of the Italian metalworkers' union FIOM, Claudio Sabattini, and the personnel director of Fiat's automobiles division, Maurizio Magnabosco, is germane here. After

Sabattini had argued the union's line of 'negotiated co-operation' (*cooperazione contrattata*), a line which acknowledged the existence of a conflictual relation between capital and labour, Magnabosco replied stressing the harshness of a competition in which everyone's fate was at stake: 'In this war, products and producers are the pawns in a game that is beyond anyone's control; they are secondary to the final objective which is profitability, the relationship between turnover and profits. In this war, Fiat calls for total commitment from its workers. Without it, there is a danger the company will disappear and the work will disappear with it.' Quoted by Paolo Griseri in *Il Manifesto*, 28 November 1995, p. 31.

10   Coriat, *L'Atelier et le robot*, p. 230. This remark applies particularly to the forms of lean production introduced in the West after the publication of Womack, *The Machine that Changed the World*. What one saw in that process was an extension neither of the Toyota system, nor of the autonomous group working introduced by Volvo first at Kalmar and subsequently at Uddevalla. It was, rather, a combination of teamwork and authoritarian command, applied first by GM in California (NUMMI), then by CAMI (GM/Suzuki joint venture) in Canada and Nissan in Britain. The CAMI management was then called in by Opel (GM's German subsidiary) to organize a brand new factory at Eisenach. In none of the factories where lean production has been introduced can there be said to have been any abolition of Taylorism, standardized assembly-line work or the dictatorship of the stopwatch. According to the surveys and studies assembled by Thomas Murakami, the intensification of work everywhere ran up against resistance from the workforce. This expressed itself, among other things, in the rejection of '*kaizen*', that is to say, a refusal to make proposals for improving the quality of the product or gaining higher productivity. Proposals were parachuted in by the supervisory staff or (at Eisenach) made obligatory on pain of loss of bonuses.

11   Coriat draws a distinction between three models of involvement: 'imposed', 'incentivized' and 'negotiated' involvement. To my knowledge, Volvo Uddevalla has been the only example of truly negotiated involvement, the German examples being more of the order of incentivized involvement. At Opel Eisenach, in particular, the workers lose their bonuses if they do not suggest three improvements per month.

12   Jean-Pierre Durand, 'L'innovation brimée', in J.-P. Durand (ed.), *La Fin du modèle suédois*, Syros, Paris, 1994, p. 122. Durand stresses that the Uddevallian model of 'holistic assembly' 'is diametrically opposed to Toyota's lean production' adopted shortly afterwards by all the world's car producers.

13   This, as we saw above, was the ambition of the 'Meidner Plan'.

14   I stress that they are met only in part because Durand, on whom I draw to a considerable degree in this account, stresses that we should not form an idealized vision of what it was like to work at Uddevalla. That factory might well have been the best that could be done in terms of self-management of the immediate production process and far superior to the reality of the Toyotist model. Yet, argues Durand, we should not see the

'holistic approach' as a 'new panacea: even when done on a long cycle, assembly work is repetitive and the element of creativity which could give a meaning to the work remains minor. There is certainly less rejection of work in holistic shops than Toyotan ones, but the job satisfaction of the assembly workers at Uddevalla or Kalmar does not seem to live up to the hopes of the advocates of the organic or holistic method. In other words, though the work is not as attractive as predicted, it is considerably less unpleasant than elsewhere.' Durand, 'L'innovation brimée', p. 128.

15 I defined the three conditions in question in André Gorz, *Critique of Economic Reason*, Verso, London, 1989, pp. 78–81.

16 P. Zariffian, 'Le travail: de l'opération à l'action', in J. Bidet and J. Texier (eds), *La Crise du travail*, Actuel Marx/PUF, Paris, 1994, p. 205.

17 I have found a particularly happy formulation of this antagonism, not much thematized in the Marxist tradition, in the writings of Jacques Bidet. 'Work,' he writes, 'finds itself *mobilized* towards ends [which] are particular to the person exerting economic power, and *polarized* by the conditions for maintaining that power. This question . . . relates not only to the apportionment of the product, but to the nature, possible use and meaning of what is produced and, therefore, also to the conditions of constraint and meaning in which production is carried on.' 'Meaning is conferred upon work in the relationship . . . between the effort or exertion it requires and the social *meaning* of production: "real abstraction" is thwarted to the extent that those whose work is propelled toward "abstract" goals manage to impose the production of a true social utility, an authentic cultural meaning." J. Bidet, 'Le travail fait époque', in Bidet and Texier, *La Crise du travail*, pp. 251, 254. See also J. Bidet, *Théorie de la modernité*, PUF, Paris, 1990, pp. 196–209.

18 Durand, 'L'innovation brimée', pp. 127, 131.

19 Marco Bascetta, *Nuove servitù*, Manifesto libri, Rome, 1994, p. 10.

20 Marco Revelli, 'Economia e modello sociale nel passagio tra fordismo e toyotismo', in P. Ingrao and R. Rossanda (eds), *Appuntamento di fine secolo*, Manifesto libri, Rome, 1995, p. 191.

21 Paolo Virno, *Mondanità*, Manifesto libri, Rome, 1995, pp. 80, 94, 97.

22 Maurizio Lazzarato, 'Le concept de travail immatériel: la grande entreprise', *Futur antérieur*, 10, 1992, pp. 59–60.

23 See *Critique of Economic Reason*, pp. 92–3, 95, 98–9.

24 'The workers are no longer – and will less and less be – interchangeable bearers of physical energy, whose labour power is of value only insofar as it is used and alienated by the person who purchases it from them and combines it externally with other undifferentiated forces. Labour is no longer a quantity of time and energy, but a praxis conscious of its autonomy, bearing within it its own sovereign demands. [The labour power of the workers] in the advanced industries . . . is from the outset of value only by its own capacity to organize its relations with the powers of others.

In those industries, the worker is literally impossible to command . . . [His] work is apprehended immediately as being not only the production of a pre-determinate *thing*, but, first and foremost, the production of a *rela-*

tionship between workers. Alienation within work is tending to disappear, but the alienation of work subsists, and is tending to become unbearable by virtue of the limits and final orientation the concern for profitability imposes on sovereign praxis . . .

The demand for self-management, which arises out of productive praxis, cannot stop at the factory gates, or at the doors of the laboratories or research establishments . . . People who cannot be ordered about in their working lives will not be ordered about indefinitely in their lives as citizens, nor subjected to the decisions of central administrations.' André Gorz, *Stratégie ouvrière et néocapitalisme*, Le Seuil, Paris, 1964, ch. 5.

25 M. Lazzarato and Antonio Negri, 'Travail immatériel et subjectivité', *Futur antérieur*, 6, pp. 95–6.

26 Michael Hardt and A. Negri, *Labor of Dionysos: A Critique of the State-form*, University of Minnesota Press, Minneapolis/London, 1994, p. 282.

27 Lazzarato and Negri, 'Travail immatériel et subjectivité', p. 95; M. Hardt and A. Negri, *Il lavoro di Dioniso*, Manifesto libri, Rome, 1995, pp. 113–14.

28 Zariffian, 'Le travail: de l'opération à l'action', pp. 204–5.

29 Ibid., pp. 199–201.

30 P. Virno, 'Quelques notes à propos du *general intellect*', *Futur antérieur*, 10, 1992, pp. 48–9.

31 Virno, ibid, p. 52. 'This has reached the point where "freedom of expression" today means "abolition of wage labour",' adds Virno, neglecting the fact that the opposite actually applies and waged labour is being abolished in favour of so-called freelance work, which consists, for the workers, in 'selling themselves' without any employer as intermediary. I shall return to this point below.

32 For all those who, following Bernard Perret, J.-L. Laville and B. Eme, claim that I regard any activity of service to persons as a servile activity in which one sells oneself, I should here make clear that we may speak of a sale of self only when its primary goal is the remuneration of one's *submission to another's will*. Professional services – particularly of care and personal assistance – provided in another person's interest are clearly not of this order. Though the therapist, the care-worker or the teacher do indeed act in the interests of the persons put in their charge, in no sense do they submit to their will or pleasure. They are supposed, rather, to understand the needs of their patients, clients or students better than those persons themselves and to act according to procedures and a code of professional ethics, adherence to which gives them formal control over the worker–client relationship. It is within the limits of a relationship marked out and objectivized by the professional procedures it entails that the therapist, the teacher, etc. serve the interests or needs of others. They are not there to do as their patients or students wish and these latter are not accorded the right or power to define what is to be done for them. Professionals are in a position of dominance. Their professionalism and the procedural rules they apply protect them from the personalization of their relations with patients or students and against collusion, compassion or other emotional ties with them. Payment for their services contributes to maintaining a dis-

tance between them and their patients or students and to giving relations between them a somewhat impersonal character – or to reducing and relativizing the personal dimension of those relations.

This is both the strength and the weakness of professional relationships. Professionalism and the dominant position it confers on the provider of a service protect that person from the desires of his/her clients and against being reduced to servant status. Payment de-personalizes the relationship and limits the debt of gratitude owed by the person assisted or treated. But the latter – and this is the other side of the coin – cannot ask for or expect concern, affection or spontaneous devotion from the professional. In short, he/she cannot expect an unconditional giving of self. Cf. *Critique of Economic Reason*, pp. 138, 141–2, 146–50, 154–5.

33 Revelli, 'Economia e modello sociale nel passagio tra fordismo e toyotismo', p. 192.

34 C. Wright Mills, *White Collar*, Oxford University Press, Oxford, 1951, pp. 182–8.

35 *Die Zeit*, 20 October 1995.

36 A. Lebaube, 'Taylor n'est pas mort', *Le Monde initiatives*, 4 December 1991.

37 See *WSI Mitteilungen*, 3, 1986, Düsseldorf. I summarized Lecher's article in *Critique of Economic Reason*, pp. 67–8. WSI is the research institute of the German trade-union confederation (DGB).

38 Michael Hammer and James Champy, *Reengineering the Corporation. A Manifesto for Business Revolution*, HarperCollins, New York, 1993.

39 *Wall Street Journal*, 19–20 March 1993.

40 This is the prediction of Heinrich Henzler, head of McKinsey Germany, and Lothar Späth, chairman of Jenoptik AG (formerly Zeiss Jena), in *Sind die Deutschen noch zu retten?*, Bertelsmann, Munich, 1993. In fact, between 1991 and 1996, the total number of jobs in Germany fell by 2.6 million.

41 V. William Bridges, *How to Prosper in a World Without Jobs*, Allen and Unwin, London, pp. viii, 160.

42 Denis Poulot, *Le Sublime*, La Découverte, Paris, 1980.

43 On this subject, see Sergio Bologna, 'Durée du travail et postfordisme', *Futur antérieur*, 35/36, 1996.

44 Cf. Juliet Schor, *The Overworked American*, Basic Books, New York, 1992.

45 Manfred Bischoff, 'L'humanité a-t-elle toujours "travaillé"?', in 'Crise du travail, crise de civilisation', *Théologiques*, 2 (3), October 1995, Montreal.

Chpater 3 The Lost Magic of Work

1 For more details, see André Gorz, *Critique of Economic Reason*, Verso, London, 1989, pp. 13–15.

2 Renaud Sainsaulieu, 'Quel avenir pour le travail?', *Esprit*, December 1995.

3 Cf. Rainer Zoll, *Alltagssolidarität und Individualismus, Zum soziokulturellen Wandel*, Suhrkamp, Frankfurt, 1993.

4   Cf. Paul Grell and Anne Wéry, *Héros obscurs de la précarité*, L'Harmattan, Paris, 1993.
5   Cf. Karl H. Hörnig, Annette Gerhard and Mathis Michailow, *Zeitpioniere. Flexible Arbeitszeiten, neuer Lebensstil*, Suhrkamp, Frankfurt, 1990.
6   Grell and Wéry, *Héros obscurs de la précarité*, p. 164.
7   Daniel Yankelovich, *New Rules – Searching for Self-fulfillment in a World Turned Upside Down*, Random House, New York, 1981. A major survey carried out by Yankelovich in 1990 showed that 58 per cent of young people between 18 and 29 take the view that a job which doesn't give you complete satisfaction isn't worth doing, except very temporarily.
8   Rainer Zoll, *Nicht so wie unsere Eltern*, Westdeutscher Verlag, Opladen, 1989.
9   David Coupland, *Generation X. Tales for an Accelerated Culture*, St Martin's Press, New York, 1991, p. 29.
10 Finn Bowring, Ph.D. thesis, University of Lancaster, 1996, p. 327. Bowring is summarizing the findings of David Cannon's study, *Generation X and the New Work Ethic*, Demos, London, 1994. The quotations are from p. 13 of that document.
11 Alain Lebaube, 'Premier travail', *Le Monde initiatives*, 22 January 1992.
12 Alain Lebaube, 'L'élite des grandes écoles est fatiguée', *Le Monde initiatives*, 23 January 1991.
13 Alain Lebaube, 'La mutation du travail', *Le Monde initiatives*, 11 May 1994.
14 Ibid.
15 J.-L. Patané, a freelance computer programmer, declares significantly: 'If I set up my own company one day, as soon as the money starts coming in, I'll put in a manager and get the hell out of there.' Florian Rochat, *La Saga du boulot*, Pierre-Marcel Favre, Lausanne/Paris, 1986.
16 *Gallup Monthly*, September 1991.
17 Yankelovich, 'Young Adult Europe' [1994], *Yankelovich Monitor*, 1971–95.
18 Cited by Roger Sue, *Temps et ordre social*, PUF, Paris, 1994.
19 According to the *British Social Attitudes Survey* of 1993, cited by Roy Pahl, 'Finding Time to Live', *Demos*, 5, 1995.
20 Juliet Schor, 'The New American Dream', *Demos*, 5, 1995, p. 30.
21 Hence the apparent contradiction between the answers given in opinion polls: on the one hand, a large majority of French people said (in late 1996) that it would be a 'bad thing' if 'work' took up less of a place in everyone's life. On the other, a large majority said they were in favour of the four-day week and of retirement at 55 (61 per cent).
22 This point was stressed in Échange et Projets, *La Révolution du temps choisi*, Fayard, Paris, 1980.
23 Alain Touraine, *Critique of Modernity*, trans. David Macey, Blackwell, Oxford/Cambridge, MA, 1995, pp. 233, 325.
24 Ibid., p. 274.
25 Ibid., p. 353.
26 Anthony Giddens, 'What's Left for Labour', *New Statesman and Society*, 30 September 1994, p. 40.

27 J.-L. Laville, 'La crise de la condition salariale', *Esprit*, December 1995, p. 37.

28 See Gorz, *Critique of Economic Reason*, pp. 176–9.

29 'To have a society of labourers, it is of course not necessary that every member actually be a labourer or worker . . . but only that all members consider whatever they do primarily as a way to sustain their own lives and those of their families', wrote Hannah Arendt, *The Human Condition*, University of Chicago Press, Chicago, 1958, p. 46.

30 Touraine, *Critique of Modernity*, p. 374.

31 Joffre Dumazedier, *La Révolution culturelle du temps libre, 1968–88*, Méridiens-Klincksieck, Paris, 1989, p. 139.

32 Bernard Perret, *L'Avenir du travail*, Le Seuil, Paris, 1995, pp. 122–3.

33 Bernard Ginisty, *Le Temps libéré*, Cépaduès Éditions, Toulouse, 1995.

34 As Perret envisages in *L'Avenir du travail*, p. 197.

35 Cf. the unforgettable description by C. Wright Mills: 'In a society of employees, dominated by the marketing mentality, it is inevitable that a personality market should arise. For in the great shift from manual skill to the art of "handling," selling and servicing people, personal or even intimate traits of the employee are drawn into the sphere of exchange and become of commercial relevance, become commodities in the labour market. Whenever there is a transfer of control over one individual's personal traits to another for a price, a sale of those traits which affect one's impressions upon others, a personality market arises . . .

Kindness and friendliness become aspects of personalized service or of public relations of big firms, rationalized to further the sale of something. With anonymous insincerity the Successful Person thus makes an instrument of his own appearance and personality . . . [His or her personality] must now also be managed, must become the alert yet obsequious instrument by which goods are distributed . . .

In one large department store, a planted observer said of one girl: "I have been watching her for three days now. She wears a fixed smile on her made-up face, and it never varies, no matter to whom she speaks. I never heard her laugh spontaneously or naturally . . . I myself tried to copy such an expression, but I am unable to keep such a smile on my face if it is not sincerely and genuinely motivated . . ."

Both the new entrepreneurs and the sales personalities serve the bureaucracies, and each, in his own way, practices the creative art of selling himself . . . As demand increases, public schools add courses that attempt to meet the business demand "for workers with a pleasant manner." Since business leaders hold that "a far greater percentage of personnel lose their jobs because of personality difficulties than because of inefficiency," the course features "training in attitudes of courtesy, thoughtfulness and friendliness; skills of voice control . . . et cetera."

Without common values and mutual trust, the cash nexus that links one man to another in transient contact has been made subtle in a dozen ways and made to bite deeper into all areas of life and relations. People are required by the salesman ethic and convention to pretend interest in others in order to manipulate them . . . [O]ne knows that manipulation is inherent in every human contact. Men are estranged from one another as each secretly tries to make an instrument of the other, and in time a full circle is made: one makes an instrument of himself, and is estranged from it also.' *White Collar*, Oxford University Press, Oxford, 1951, pp. 182–8.

Chapter 4 Moving Beyond Wage-Based Society

1 Commissariat général du Plan, *Le Travail dans 20 ans*, Odile Jacob/La Documentation française, Paris, 1995, pp. 30–1.
2 Ibid., pp. 286–8.
3 Ibid., p. 282.
4 Centre des jeunes dirigeants, *L'Entreprise au XXIe siècle*, Flammarion, Paris, 1996, p. 125.
5 Ibid., pp. 43–4.
6 Ibid., p. 11.
7 Ibid., p. 119–20.
8 Centre des jeunes dirigeants, *L'Entreprise au XXIe siècle*, pp. 27–8.
9 This formula, which has been very widely taken up, was coined by Claudio Napoleoni, the Catholic Communist economist and philosopher, whose critique of capitalist civilization for forty years fuelled the debates of the Italian extreme left. When, during a public debate, a heckler shouted out, 'Claudio, dovè la porta?' (Claudio, where is the exit [i.e. from capitalism]?), Napoleoni replied: 'We don't have to exit from capitalism to get to something else; but we have to widen as far as possible the difference between society and capitalism – in other words, to widen the space of non-identification of people with inverted subjectivity.'
10 Fausto Bertinotti, 'Una domanda', *Il Manifesto*, 26 January 1996.
11 Yoland Bresson, *Partage*, February–March 1995.
12 Anthony Giddens, *Beyond Left and Right. The Future of Radical Politics*, Polity Press, Cambridge, 1994.
13 Cf. André Gorz, *Paths to Paradise: On the Liberation from Work*, trans. Malcolm Imrie, Pluto Press, London, 1985, pp. 40–4.
14 Claus Offe, 'Freiwillig auf die Anteilnahme am Arbeitsmarkt verzichten', *Frankfurter Rundschau*, 19 July 1995.
15 Diane Elson, 'Market Socialism or Socialization of the Market?', *New Left Review*, 172, November–December 1988, p. 29.
16 The state of Singapore recently passed a law making it compulsory for children of elderly parents to take care of them. This led the children concerned to request attestations from their parents to the effect that they did provide care. The concern of those who spontaneously took care of their parents was thereby contaminated by an obligation to the state. As for those who do not take care of their parents, they don't have much difficulty getting their parents to sign bogus declarations.
17 In fact, at a symposium of 500 private and public decision-makers organized by the Gorbachev Foundation in September 1995, the guarantee of

a minimum subsistence income was regarded as indispensable in the long run by a large majority of the participants. In their view, the employment rate was going to fall to 20 per cent and the unemployment rate was going to rise to 80 per cent. 'Social integration will have to be achieved by charitable work in the third sector, by neighbourhood mutual aid schemes, by engaging in sport or all kinds of voluntary activity. "These activities could be given new status by the payment of a small remuneration", argues Professor Roy' (quoted by Hans-Peter Martin and Harald Schumann, *Die Globalisierungsfalle*, Rowohlt, Hamburg, 1996, pp. 12–13).

18 See Alain Caillé and Ahmet Insel, 'Vers un revenu minimum inconditionnel?', *La Revue de Mauss*, 7, 1st semester 1996, p. 13.

19 Karl Marx, *Grundrisse*, Penguin Books, Harmondsworth, 1973, p. 704.

20 André Gorz, *Strategy for Labour: A Radical Proposal*, Beacon Press, Boston, 1967, p. 117.

21 Between 1979 and 1994, German company profits rose by 90 per cent, while wages increased by 6 per cent. However, company taxation as a percentage of tax revenue fell from 35 per cent in 1960 to 25 per cent in 1980 and 13 per cent in 1994. In the same period, taxes on wages and salaries as a percentage of total tax revenue rose from 16 per cent in 1960 to 30 per cent in 1980 and 36 per cent in 1994. If company taxes had remained at 1980 levels, Germany's tax revenue would have increased by 86,000,000,000 DM instead of falling by 9 per cent. From D. Eisel and G. Erb, 'Vom Elend des kapitalistischen "Sozialstaates", *Neue Gesellschaft/ Frankfurter Hefte*, 4, 1996, p. 351.

22 Wassily W. Leontief, 'The Distribution of Work and Income', *Scientific American*, 247:3, September 1982, p. 155.

23 The *Grundrisse* was not published until 1939 (as *Rohentwurf*: rough outline) by the Marx–Engels–Lenin Institute in Moscow. The first edition available to the public was published by Dietz (Berlin) in 1953.

24 René Passet, 'La Sécu entre deux chaises', *Transversales*, 37, January–February 1996.

25 René Passet and Jacques Robin's vision in *Transversales* is of a 'plural economy *with* a market' and various types of money: one type would be capitalizable and would be of unlimited validity and convertibility; another would be 'consumption money' with a time limit on its validity and no possibility of hoarding it; there would also be local currencies which would be restricted in their circulation and convertibility and whose life-span would be short.

It was already Jacques Duboin's conception that this consumption money should be cancelled by the act of purchase it permitted. This is because it is not coming out of taxes on primary income. In an economy in which production barely distributes wages any more, it cannot be. The money by which demand is funded can only be a social money, which is issued in quantities determined by political considerations.

26 All modern states practise political pricing already. All products and services are either subsidized or taxed at very different rates (ranging from tenths of a per cent to multiples of 100 per cent). This does not prevent us from still having markets, knowledge of costs, and price competition.

27 The term 'ecosophic' was coined by Félix Guattari in *The Three Ecologies* (trans. Chris Turner, *New Formations*, 8, Summer 1989, pp. 131–47), and its meaning was developed extensively in *Chaosmose* (Galilée, 1992). A condensed definition of the term is given in Guattari's article 'Vers une "Écosophie"'. It reads: 'An "ecosophy", that is to say a perspective including ethical dimensions, and articulating together the entire range of scientific, political, environmental, social and mental ecologies, is perhaps destined to be substituted for the old ideologies which improperly sectorized the social, the private and the civil, and which were incapable of establishing connections between the political, ethical and aesthetic domains' (*Transversales Science/Culture*, 2, March–April 1990, pp. 2–3).

28 Marx, *Grundrisse*, pp. 711–12.

29 Ibid., p. 706.

30 Ibid.

31 Ibid.

32 Ibid., p. 711.

33 The 20 per cent reduction in working hours and the 16 per cent drop in net wages brought about such a rise in productivity that the move benefited the Volkswagen group considerably. The reorganization of working hours, which provided, among other things, a choice between some 150 different working patterns (i.e. a choice between 150 different ways of spreading one's working hours over the day, the week or the month), subsequently enabled further productivity gains to be made.

34 Michel Albert, *Le Pari français*, Le Seuil, Paris, 1982.

35 If it could be divided between the entire French population of working age, the current quantity of work would represent less than 800 hours per year.

36 Dominique Méda, *Le Travail. Une valeur en voie de disparition*, Aubier, Paris, 1995, pp. 182ff.

37 This is the case with those – generally much sought-after – jobs which are also a way of life and whose productivity is not measurable: all the artistic, educational and caring occupations (from gamekeeper to psychotherapist). All are diminished when they become subject to economic rationalization, to productivity norms.

38 I envisioned an educational system of this kind in 1976, combined with a universal grant akin to the French minimum wage provision. See 'A Possible Utopia', in *Ecology as Politics*, Pluto Press, London/South End Press, Boston, 1980, pp. 42–50, reprinted (as 'Utopia for a Possible Dual Society') in *Farewell to the Working Class*, Pluto Press, London, 1982, pp. 145–52.

39 R. Zoll, 'Staatsbürgereinkommen für Sozialdienste', in O. Negt (ed.), *Die zweite Gesellschaftsreform*, Steidl, Göttingen, 1994, pp. 91–4.

40 On this, see Michel Hervé, mayor of Parthenay, 'Citoyenneté active et développement urbain durable. L'expérience de Parthenay', *Transversales*, 41, September–October 1996. On 'ecosophic town planning', see especially the lavishly illustrated work by Léon Krier, *Architecture, choix ou fatalité*, Norma, Paris, 1996.

41 Félix Guattari, 'La cité subjective'. From the text of a lecture delivered in 1992 at UNESCO, Paris. Print-outs of the undated and unpublished type-

script may be requested from Imec (Institut mémoire de l'édition contemporaine), 9 rue Bline, 75009 Paris ('Fonds Guattari').

42 For a history of LETS and their precursors in the 1920s and 1930s, see the work by Claus Offe and Rolf Heinze cited below. For a list and brief description of the various British LETS, their initial difficulties and the solutions they found to them, see Helen Barnes, Peter North and Perry Walker, 'LETS on Low Income', in *New Economics*, New Economics Foundation, London, 1996, 38 pages.

  Information and practical advice are available from LETSLink, LETS Development Agency, 2, Kent Street, Portsmouth, Hants PO1 3BS.

  On the general philosophy of LETS, see the excellent article by Martine Brissac, 'Les semences du changement', in 'Tout travail, non-travail, histoire de FOUS', *Le Temps libéré*, Maison Partage, Cépaduès Éditions, Toulouse, 1995, pp. 151–60.

43 Claus Offe and Rolf Heinze, *Organisierte Eigenarbeit. Das Modell Kooperationsring*, Campus Verlag, Frankfurt, 1990.

44 The most developed schemes do, however, tend to make exceptions to the principle of equivalence in order to attract or retain those members with relatively rare skills: accountants, computer specialists, medical personnel, music teachers, etc. One hour of their work entitles them to two or three hours of the more common services. For a critical discussion of the social rules which ought to govern exchanges in a modern, classless, socialist society, see the remarkable essay by Carmen Sirianni, 'Classless Society', *Socialist Review*, 59, San Francisco, September–October 1981, especially the section 'Historical materialism and the exchange of labor'. Among these rules, Sirianni cites: '(1) a basic pluralism of options for the social and technical organization of various areas of production . . . ; (2) a basic pluralism of options for the individual fulfillment of one's share of socially necessary labor; and (3) the systematic distribution of life opportunities (creative work, free time etc.) in a relatively egalitarian manner. Given the various types of work to be done and their different social and technical organization, we must also allow for the possibility that differential weight may be assigned to various jobs in the calculation of contributions to socially necessary labor (e.g., jobs that are particularly unpleasant, inconvenient or hazardous, or that can't be widely rotated). In any case, these goals necessitate the development of standards for the exchange of necessary labor, standards through which contributions of social labor can be made commensurate . . . Indeed, the very meaning of "equality" in a classless society is linked to the articulation of such standards.'

45 See André Gauron, *Les Remparts de l'argent*, Odile Jacob, Paris, 1991, pp. 47ff.

46 Nordal Åkerman, 'Can Sweden be Shrunk?', *Development Dialogue*, 2, 1972, pp. 91–2.

47 Frithjof Bergmann teaches philosophy at the University of Michigan, Ann Arbor, and has worked for some ten years with adolescents, the unemployed and homeless people in New York and Detroit. Beginning from the obvious starting point that waged work itself will in future structure the

life of the majority of the population less and less, he suggests organizing that life into three separate time zones in which they move between three types of activity: the time of paid work; the time of high-tech self-providing – that is to say of production for self supported by advanced technologies; and the time in which you do what you most enjoy – the time for what I have called autonomous activities, which are done for their own sake alone.

In Bergmann's vision, each of these three activities is to occupy two days a week (though more flexible formulas are not to be ruled out). Among the self-providing activities his centre organizes in Detroit, Bergmann mentions the construction of 18–20-storey buildings, self-built by people in poor housing conditions, to live in themselves. These are built under professional supervision, using ecologically sound materials and the most advanced construction techniques. Other people make their own clothing, shoes and leather jackets, 'which is child's play using computerized sewing machines'.

'Our aim,' says Bergmann, 'is to self-provide 70–80 per cent of the things we need for our lives, without expending much labour' and to do away with the exhausting monotony of full-time work, which you find, for example, in the clothing industry. '"New work" means: a more creative, imaginative, personal and meaningful range of activities.' From an interview with Erika Martens in *Die Zeit*, 7 March 1997, p. 27. It also means, Bergmann added in his lectures, 'to liberate work from the tyranny of the job'.

48　Cf. Claus Haeffner, *Mensch und Computer im Jahr 2000*, Birkhäuser, Zurich, 1988.

49　Offe and Heinze, *Organisierte Eigenarbeit*, p. 75.

50　Ibid., p. 75, pp. 342–4; J. Jessen, *Arbeit nach der Arbeit*, Westdeutscher Verlage, Opladen, 1988, p. 277.

51　Jacques Bidet presents an excellent theoretical critique of the 'Marxian utopia of the abolition of the division of labour', of the abolition of the market and the abolition of the state in his *Théorie de la modernité*, PUF, Paris, 1990. See especially pp. 295–305.

52　R. Land, 'Ökosteuer oder Ökokapital', *Andere Zeiten*, 4, Berlin, 1994. This article gave rise to a debate in later numbers of the journal.

53　A movement which originated in the Netherlands in 1994 provides a good illustration of the capacity of co-operative communities to develop, through networking, an activity which connects local and universal concerns in a two-way feedback loop, reflecting the watchword, 'Think globally, act locally.' This movement, which had been developing for several years, emerged against a backdrop of general anxiety about global warming. Since this would cause sea levels to rise, it threatens considerable areas of Dutch territory with submersion. To slow down or halt global warming (in so far as it is due to the greenhouse effect), the consumption of fossil fuels has to fall.

To achieve such a fall, it is more effective, and of greater political impact, to demonstrate that we can live better, while consuming less, than it is to resort to fiscal and/or authoritarian measures. On the initiative of a core group of scientists, architects and citizens, so-called 'eco-teams' were formed in dozens of towns and cities of the Netherlands to try out new styles of life and new types of environment, combining savings in energy, sharing of resources, pooling of equipment, exchanges of services, etc. The eco-teams meet once a month, decide priorities and compare their results and methods with those of other teams. Emulation in frugality, conviviality and less hurried living, all seen as factors of a better 'quality of life', overturns the values of the 'consumer society', and micro-social initiatives receive social recognition and appreciation for their general significance in the definition of a novel life-style and a new type of society. The growing part played by self-providing with a public purpose reduces the role of abstract labour and commodity consumption in the satisfaction and, above all, the determination of needs, and promotes the definition of a standard of 'adequacy' through ongoing choice between the various determinants of the quality of life (for more details, see *Der Spiegel*, 13, Hamburg, 1995).

The aspiration to autonomy, self-determination and self-reliance, on the part of both communities and persons, and to the full development of their capacities and relations, is a common value in the pursuit of the 'common good' and the cultural basis of both social recognition and social criticism. Rather than being forms of sacrifice and asceticism, self-restraint and frugality become gratifying, and highly regarded, ways of affirming personal autonomy and pursuing the full development and sovereignty of persons and communities. We are a long way here, then, from 'social usefulness' – that is, from a social morality in which the individual is socially recognized for the way his/her work and function *serve* society, regarded as a kind of totalizing subject. Society becomes the linkage between forms of perpetually renewed, self-produced, communitarian sociality and collective public services, infrastructures and mega-tools which complement, sustain and facilitate the self-production of sociality in concrete labour.

Epilogue

1 Adret, *Travailler deux heures par jour*, Le Seuil, Paris, 1977. A follow-up volume entitled *Résister* was published under the same name by the Éditions de Minuit in early 1997.
2 'Die Humanität des Menschen' was the term used by Günther Stern, alias Günther Anders, the precursor in the 1950s of militant political ecology and the critique of technology. See *Die Antiquiertheit des Menschen*, 2 vols, C. H. Beck, Munich, 1980.
3 See, in particular, in Paul Virilio, *The Art of the Motor*, University of Minnesota Press, Minneapolis, 1995, the admirable chapter, 'From Overman to Overexcited Man'.
4 These are the words of Eric Drexler, the pioneer of nano-technologies, who believes large-scale applications of these technologies might take place around the year 2010 (*Time Magazine*, 2 December 1996).

5 Jean-Marie Vincent, 'De la gauche domestiquée à la gauche critique', *La Revue de Mauss*, 13, p. 43.

6 M. Hardt and A. Negri write of 'the new human nature coursing through our bodies': 'The cyborg is now the only model available for the theorizing of subjectivity. Bodies without organs, humans without qualities, cyborgs: these are the subjective figures produced and producing on the contemporary horizon, the subjective figures today capable of communism'. *The Labor of Dionysus*, University of Minnesota Press, Minneapolis/London, 1994, p. 14.

7 See Daniel Verrès, *Le Discours du capital*, L'Herne, Paris, 1971.

Digression 1 Community and Society

1 Jean-Marc Ferry, *Les Puissances de l'expérience*, vol. 2, Le Cerf, Paris, 1991, pp. 163, 164.

2 Serge Latouche, *La Planète des naufragés*, La Découverte, Paris, 1993.

3 Alain de Benoist, 'Communautairiens vs. libéraux', *Krisis*, 16, June 1994, p. 4.

4 Ibid., pp. 4–5. The passage quoted by de Benoist is from Chantal Mouffe, 'La citoyenneté et la critique de la raison libérale', in J. Poulain and P. Vermeeren (eds), *L'Identité philosophique européenne*, L'Harmattan-Association Descartes, Paris, 1993, p. 101.

5 Quoted by Otto Kallscheuer in his preface to Michael Walzer, *Zivile Gesellschaft und amerikanische Demokratie*, Rotbuch, Hamburg, 1992.

6 One should not forget, however, that both the *Heimat* and the life-world can be lost. They are preserved only thanks to the stability and continuity of the original way of life, the permanence of places and landscapes, techniques and customs, and relations to the surrounding world.

7 Michael Walzer: 'Under conditions of security, I will acquire a more complex identity than the idea of tribalism suggests. I will identify myself with more than one tribe: I will be an American, a Jew, an Easterner, an intellectual, a professor'. 'Notes on the New Tribalism', *Dissent*, Spring 1992, p. 171.

8 Cf. the following phrase in Khaled Kelkal's remarkable statement to *Le Monde* in October 1995: 'I am neither French nor Algerian, I am a Muslim'.

9 Cf. Dick Howard, 'Rediscovering the Left', *Praxis International*, January 1991; *Defining the Political*, Macmillan, London, 1989.

10 Michael Walzer, 'Für eine Politik der Differenz', in *Zivile Gesellschaft und amerikanische Demokratie*, pp. 235–6.

11 Ibid.

12 De Benoist, 'Communautairiens vs. libéraux', pp. 15–16.

13 'Three Interviews with Alain de Benoist', *Telos*, 98–9, Winter 1993–Spring 1994, p. 174. The interview cited was carried out by *Le Monde*, but was never published in France.

14 I shall return to this question at greater length with reference to

Habermas, demonstrating the incompatibility between his conception of the life-world and his understanding of communicative reason.

15 Étienne Tassin, 'L'Europe, une communauté politique?', *Esprit*, November 1991.

16 Cf. Alain Touraine, *Qu'est-ce que la démocratie?*, Fayard, Paris, 1994, especially the chapter 'La politique du sujet'.

Digression 2   Alain Touraine or the Subject of Criticism

1 A. Touraine, *Critique of Modernity*, Oxford, Blackwell, 1995, pp. 97–8, 99.

2 J. Habermas, *Theorie des kommunikativen Handelns*, vol. 2, Suhrkamp, Frankfurt, 1981, pp. 273ff, 455. [The wording adopted here is André Gorz's own translation: Trans.]

3 Ibid., pp. 258, 228, 461, 581.

4 Touraine, *Critique of Modernity*, p. 242.

5 Ibid., p. 231.

6 Ibid., pp. 214, 205.

7 See J. Habermas, 'Diskursethik – Notizen zu einem Begründungsprogramm', *Moralbewusstsein und kommunikatives Handeln*, Suhrkamp, Frankfurt, 1983, pp. 53ff.

8 A. Touraine, *Qu'est-ce que la démocratie?*, Fayard, Paris, 1994, p. 179.

9 Ibid., p. 178.

10 Habermas, *Theorie des kommunikativen Handelns*, vol. 2, pp. 277–8.

11 Ibid., p. 228.

12 Ibid., pp. 550, 566.

13 A. Schütz and T. Luckmann, *Strukturen der Lebenswelt*, Suhrkamp, Frankfurt, 1979.

14 Habermas, *Theorie des kommunikativen Handelns*, vol. 2, pp. 189, 198–9, 205.

15 See A. Honneth, *Kritik der Macht: Reflexionsstufen einer kritischen Gesellschaftstheorie*, Suhrkamp, Frankfurt, 1985; 'Von der Aktualität des Adornoschen Denkens: Ein Gespräch mit Axel Honneth und Hans Ernst Schiller', *Links*, 7/8, 1994, pp. 27–31; 'Die soziale Dynamik von Missachtung: Zur Ortsbestimmung einer kritischen Gesellschaftstheorie', in C. Görg (ed.), *Gesellschaft im Übergang*, Wissenschaftliche Buchgemeinschaft, Darmstadt, 1994.

16 Touraine, *Critique of Modernity*, p. 260.

17 Ibid., p. 251.

18 Ibid., p. 160.

19 Ibid., p. 163.

20 Ibid., p. 244.

21 Ibid.

22 Ibid.

23 Ibid., p. 245.

24 Ibid.

25 Ibid., p. 251.

26 A. Touraine, *Le Retour de l'acteur*, Fayard, Paris, 1984, pp. 49–50.
27 Touraine, *Critique of Modernity*, p. 288.
28 A. Touraine, *Mouvements sociaux d'aujourd'hui: acteurs et analystes*, Éditions Ouvrières, Paris, 1982.
29 E. Fromm, *Escape from Freedom*, Rinehart, New York, 1942.
30 J.-P. Sartre, *Being and Nothingness*, trans. Hazel Barnes, Philosophical Library, New York, 1956.
31 Touraine, *Critique of Modernity*, p. 235.
32 Ibid., pp. 243, 242.
33 Ibid., p. 275.
34 Ibid., pp. 280, 274.
35 Ibid., p. 361.
36 Ibid., p. 352.
37 Ibid., pp. 314–15.
38 Ibid., p. 282.
39 Ibid., p. 353.
40 Ibid., p. 231.
41 Ibid., p. 279.
42 Ibid., p. 167.
43 Sartre, *The Transcendence of the Ego*, trans. Forrest Williams and Robert Kirkpatrick, Noonday Press, New York, 1957; *Being and Nothingness*.
44 Touraine, *Critique of Modernity*, p. 230.
45 Ibid., p. 229.
46 Ibid., p. 273.
47 Ibid., p. 274. Italics in original.
48 Ibid., pp. 226–7.
49 A. Giddens, *Modernity and Self-Identity: Self and Society in the Late Modern Age*, Polity Press, Cambridge, 1991.
50 Touraine, *Critique of Modernity*, p. 264.
51 Ibid., p. 218.
52 Ibid., p. 233.
53 See ibid., pp. 300ff.
54 Giddens, *Modernity and Self-Identity*, p. 81.
55 R. Zoll, H. Bents, H. Brauer, J. Flieger, E. Neumann and M. Oechsle, *Nicht so wie unsere Eltern: Ein neues kulturelles Modell?*, Westdeutscher Verlag, Opladen, 1989.
56 Touraine, *Critique of Modernity*, p. 183.
57 Giddens, *Modernity and Self-Identity*, p. 209.
58 Touraine, *Critique of Modernity*, p. 192.
59 Ibid., p. 304.
60 Ibid., pp. 296ff.
61 Ibid., p. 296.
62 Touraine, *Qu'est-ce que la démocratie?*, p. 171.
63 Touraine, *Critique of Modernity*, p. 219.
64 Ibid., p. 374.
65 Ibid., p. 220.
66 Touraine, *Qu'est-ce que la démocratie?*, p. 263.

67 Ibid., pp. 159, 200.
68 Touraine, *Critique of Modernity*, p. 222.
69 J.-M. Vincent, *Critique du travail*, PUF, Paris, 1987, pp. 19–20.
70 Ibid., p. 361.
71 Ibid., p. 371.

Index